RHODODENDRONS

WITH

CAMELLIAS and MAGNOLIAS
2000

GW00370476

THE ROYAL
HORTICULTURAL
SOCIETY

Published in 2000 by
The Royal Horticultural Society,
80 Vincent Square, London SW1P 2PE

ISBN 1 874431 97 3

Edited for the RHS by Karen Wilson

Honorary Editor for the Rhododendron, Camellia and Magnolia Group
Philip Evans

Editorial Subcommittee
Maurice Foster
Rosemary Foster
Brian Wright

Printed by Embassy Press, London and Crowborough, Sussex

CONTENTS

CHAIRMAN'S FOREWORD 5

EDITORIAL 7

50 YEARS OF CAMELLIAS AT
MARWOOD HILL
by Dr James Smart 9

THE SPECIES OF THE BARBATUM
ALLIANCE
by David Chamberlain 14

E H WILSON – THE MAGNOLIA
LEGACY
by Maurice Foster 18

THE 1953 EXPEDITION TO THE
N BURMA TRIANGLE
by U Chit Ko Ko
Foreword by Jean Kingdon Ward 25

THE PROPAGATION OF
RHODODENDRONS FROM CUTTINGS
by E G Millais 38

THE RESTORATION OF WENTWORTH
CASTLE GARDENS
Derek Rogers 43

THE INTERNATIONAL CAMELLIA
CONGRESS
by Joey Warren 48

PHOTOGRAPHIC COMPETITION 52

THE REBIRTH OF *MAGNOLIA
SARGENTIANA* VAR. *ROBUSTA* AT
HIGH BEECHES
by Anne Boscawen 53

THE HARDY HYBRID COLLECTION
by Miranda Gunn and John Bond 55

ALAN HARDY VMH
by John Bond 59

SIR GILES LODER BT, VMH
by John Bond 61

RHODODENDRON GROUP TOUR -
EAST AND WEST SUSSEX,
6-10 MAY, 1999
by Cynthia Postan 62

THE RHODODENDRON AND
CAMELLIA COMPETITIONS
The Early Rhododendron Show
by David Farnes 67

The Main Rhododendron Show – Species
by Archie Skinner 69

The Main Rhododendron Show – Hybrids
by Brian Wright 71

The Early Camellia Competition
by Cicely Perring 74

The Main Camellia Show
by Cicely Perring 75

AWARDS 78

BOOK REVIEW 81

COMMITTEES 82

INDEX 85

COLOURED ILLUSTRATIONS

Front cover: Rhododendron augustinii.
Exbury's winning entry for Class 21 at the 1999 Main Rhododendron Competition.

Back cover (top): Camellia 'Wild Fire' winner of Class 13 for D R Strauss at the1999 Early Camellia Competition. *(Middle) R. sutchuenense.* An entry at the Early Rhododendron Competition 1999. *(Bottom): Magnolia campbellii* var. *mollicomata* 'Werrington' at P van Veen's garden, Switzerland

Fig. 1: The flower and leaves of *Rhododendron barbatum* (RBG Edinburgh)
Fig. 2: R. erosum (RBG Edinburgh)
Fig. 3: R. exasperatum showing the typical long bristles of the leaf stalk (RBG Edinburgh)
Fig. 4: Magnolia 'Galaxy' (Maurice Foster)
Fig. 5: M. dawsoniana.(Maurice Foster)
Fig. 6: M. sprengeri 'Copeland Court' (Maurice Foster)
Fig. 7: M. wilsonii (Maurice Foster)
Fig. 8: U Chit Ko Ko, author of the paper on the 1953 Kingdon Ward expedition to the N Burma Triangle (David Sayers Photolibrary)
Fig. 9-12: Rhododendron propagation from cuttings (E G Millais)
Fig. 13: Wentworth Castle Gardens (Derek Rogers)
Fig. 14: R. 'Queen of Hearts' (Photos Great Britain)
Fig. 15: Camellias as Ikebana (Cynthia Postan)
Fig. 16: R. yakushimanum on Mt Miyanoura, Yakushima Island (H Hiromori)
Fig. 17: Camellia amplexicaule (Cynthia Postan)
Fig. 18: Flowers of the High Beeches *M. sargentiana* var. *robusta* (Anne Boscawen)
Fig. 19: The 'reborn' *M. sargentiana* var. *robusta* at TheHigh Beeches (Anne Boscawen)
Fig. 20: Members of the Wessex Branch of the group assembled for planting at Ramster (Miranda Gunn)
Fig. 21: The pond area of the garden at Ramster (Miranda Gunn)
Fig. 22: The winner of the 2000 Photographic Competition, *R niveum* 'Crown Equerry' (J D Bottle)
Fig. 23: Second in the Photographic Competition, *Magnolia* 'Greta Eisenhut' (M. J-P Chatelard)
Fig. 24: Third equal in the Photographic competition, *R. taggianum* 'Harry Tagg' (Dr G Hargreaves)
Fig. 25: Third equal in the Photographic Competition, *R. bureavii* (J D Bottle)
Fig. 26: R. 'Our Kate' (Photos Great Britain)
Fig. 27: R. argyrophyllum 'Chinese Silver' (Photos Great Britain)
Fig. 28: Camellia 'Janet Waterhouse' (Photos Great Britain)
Fig. 29: C. 'Julia Hamiter' (Photos Great Britain)
Fig. 30: C. 'Augusto Pinto' (Photos Great Britain)
Fig. 31: C.'Mrs D. W. Davies' (Photos Great Britain)
Fig. 32: R. 'New Comet' × *R. caloxanthum* (Mrs J Arblaster)

BLACK AND WHITE ILLUSTRATIONS
p.15: Distribution map of the Barbatum Alliance
p.25 Mr and Mrs Frank Kingdon Ward
p.31: Sketch map of the North Burma Triangle and the area of the 1953 expedition
p.59: Alan Hardy VMH (Daily Telegraph)

FOREWORD

JOHN BOND

Welcome to the first Year Book of the new Millennium. I wonder if gardening as it is today and our beloved rhododendron will feature at the end of it? No further comment!

Once again my thanks are due to our Editor, Philip Evans, for gathering together a range of excellent articles on our three genera. My thanks are also due to our contributors for all of their hardwork. I would also like to extend my thanks to those advertising with us; your support is much appreciated.

I have been concerned for some time now as to the apparent lessening of interest in the rhododendron. The Rhododendron Societies throughout the world are, at best, holding firm as far as membership is concerned (as I am glad to say our group is), and at worst losing membership in spite of providing an excellent service.

While I am very aware of the problems outlined briefly above, the matter was brought home to me recently in a rather forceful way. I was attending an excellent symposium entitled 'Rooting the impossible'. The business of the day was concerned with the propagation of difficult and choice woody plants. Inevitably rhododendrons were on the agenda and on this occasion were dealt with by a very experienced propagator and wholesale grower of choice shrubs who during the course of this talk extolled the virtues of the saddle graft. Then came the punch line statement – 'not as there is much call for rhododendron grafting these days!'

So why has the demand for rhododendrons fallen away so? I do not propose to send a questionnaire to you all but I shall be grateful for helpful letters, and I will pre-empt your letters by suggesting some of the possible problems.

I have frequently heard it said that rhododendrons are only for large gardens and certainly this is true of *R. calophytum, R. fortunei,* the Loderi Group and 'Angelo' for example. However, we all know that there are legions of species and hybrids suitable for the smaller gardens. I have even heard it stated on a number of occasions that the genus is only for the wealthy garden owner. I have no wish to take that matter further.

There is of course the limiting suitable soil factor, but large areas of the British Isles offer acceptable acid soil conditions and the climatic conditions in the main are suitable.

We should look now at today's scene concerning the supply of rhododendrons and also the quality of the stock available. It is from the garden centres that most stock is purchased and these offer quite a range of *R. yakushimanum* hybrids, some hybridised in Britain and others in Germany and the USA. Almost all are produced by micropropagation in the USA and grown on in Britain by a few large wholesalers. There are also small ranges of hardy hybrids on offer, which may well have been grafted in Belgium.

That is the extent of the garden centre stock of larger rhododendrons, although the *R. yakushimanum* hybrids are fairly compact. In addition a good range of dwarf rhododendrons and an even greater selection of evergreen azaleas are stocked. These are all easily raised by cuttings here in Britain and are very much among the impulse purchases, and impulse sales are the big money spinners in the garden centres. You will all have seen the large displays of shrubs in flower inside the entrance. Lastly there are a number of glamorous deciduous Knaphill azaleas on offer but I understand demand is low for these.

So what can we learn from the garden centre stock described above? By and large it usually looks good, it is grown in three- or four-litre containers of peat-based, well-fertilised compost. There is, however, a great problem in transferring this stock into our gardens, these plants are often pot bound and the solid root ball is difficult to moisten and keep moist. I suspect also that many of these plants are placed in full exposure with no attempt to keep them cool and moist. If there are considerable losses, and I suspect that there are, the garden centre customer will look for an alternative to rhododendron for no one enjoys wasting money.

So there we are, a few suggestions as to why the rhododendron is out of favour. Do let me have your thoughts.

We do have a few, surprisingly few, specialist rhododendron nurseries who offer a range of species and choice hybrids to the discerning gardener. Of course all of our members are in that category and these specialists already have our support.

My apologies for these whinging notes but I consider the problem very important. Incidentally, if it's any consolation the demand for conifers and roses has also fallen dramatically.

Enjoy the first year of the new Millennium and keep planting. Happy woodland gardening.

EDITORIAL

PHILIP EVANS

It was David Sayers, himself a recent botanical traveller to Burma (Myanmar) who sent me a paper by his friend there, U Chit Ko Ko, written in 1953 but never published outside that country. I was struck by the clarity and topicality of this account of the rich flora of an area which it is unlikely any foreigner, since that late Kingdon Ward expedition, has been permitted to visit. It seemed so opportune to print this paper in the first Year Book of the new Millennium, as a reminder of the botanical splendour of North Burma, and also as a tribute to Frank Kingdon Ward, one of the greatest plant collectors of the century just ended.

In his book, *Return to the Irrawaddy*, Kingdon Ward described how, towards the end of the trip, he found his companion Chit Ko Ko had enscribed on a blazed tree the words 'To Mr F. Kingdon Ward who knew and loved Burma C.K.K.'. KW wrote, 'So this was Chit Ko Ko's . . . way of thanking me for having taught him some botany . . . I felt proud I should have helped to teach my young friend to appreciate the magnificent mountains of his country . . .'

Jean Rasmussen (Jean Kingdon Ward) kindly read through the text and has written a charming introduction that reveals her clear and abiding memory of those times.

Tribute to another great and prolific plant collector of this last century, is rendered by Maurice Foster in his original and meticulously researched article 'E H Wilson – the Magnolia Legacy'. Retrospection, a justifiable theme in this Millennium issue, is behind both Dr Smart's account of a half century of camellia growing at Marwood Hill, his wonderful North Devon garden and also Derek Rogers' account of the history and restoration of the gardens at Wentworth Castle, which deserve to be better known.

The double article by Miranda Gunn and John Bond, on the hardy hybrid rhododendrons, looks both backwards and forwards. A case is put forward for the need for the conservation of this historic race of garden plants, and we learn of the exciting new project commenced by our own Group, to do just that in the future.

Two other articles in this year's selection, deserve comment. While we were travelling together in south-west China two years ago, David Chamberlain told me it was time to 'clear up' the classification of the Barbata subsection of *Rhododendron*, and it is good that his conclusions are now recorded in this issue. Then Ted Millais has followed his 1999 article on propagating rhododendrons from seed, with a very useful description of the contemporary methods he recommends for successful propagation from cuttings.

Finally I would like to thank the members of the Editorial Subcommittee for their friendly assistance and support in the planning and production of this Year Book.

50 YEARS OF CAMELLIAS AT MARWOOD HILL

DR JAMES SMART

It has just occurred to me that I have been growing camellias in North Devon for the last 50 years, the latter half of the century leading up to the Millennium. When I moved to Marwood Hill in 1949 I planted my first camellia. This was given to me as a present and was very suitably called 'Donation'. This is where I learned my first lesson. I prepared the soil rather too carefully with the result that when 'Donation' was planted it sunk into the soft soil which then part covered the lower part of its trunk. The plant gradually went back and obviously was going to die. I realised the problem and removed the top layer of soil from the trunk and the plant recovered and is now some 4.5m (15ft) tall. It is a lesson which cannot be repeated often enough to the beginner that only a small covering of peat should be allowed above the root ball when you buy it in as a pot plant.

From this small beginning I have gradually increased over the years by getting in cuttings from this country and from many parts of the world so that now, in 1999, I must have nearly 1,000 camellia plants scattered in various parts of the garden as well as in a large camellia greenhouse and in several areas away from the main garden which are given over to the monoculture of the genus.

I have chiefly japonicas, reticulatas and hybrids but very few pure species.

I used to show at the camellia shows at the RHS, with some success, in classes for plants grown in the open as well as under glass. I never really enjoyed competitive growing and, later on confined myself to judging at the Vincent Square shows and for the Cornwall Society Spring shows.

I sent camellias up for awards at the shows over a number of years and got a First Class Certificate for *C. tsai* and for 'Mouchang' and Awards of Merit for a large number including 'Debbie', 'Francie L', 'Vallee Knudsen', 'White Nun', 'Matador' and 'Margaret Davis'.

For a number of years I was on the Rhododendron and Camellia Committee but resigned from this in 1997 from the point of view of age and also the distance of Barnstaple from London.

I have grown a large number of my camellias in areas away from the general garden so that they may be seen and admired in their own right without the main garden being over-stocked with one genus. I have seen too many gardens where rhododendrons have been so much in excess of any other plant or shrub that I get what I can only call 'rhododendronorrhoea', and I have been anxious that I should not get a similar situation arising from camellias. I have therefore got camellias in the main garden intermixed with rhododendrons and other shrubs, with a few isolated groups on their own.

One feature which you do not see much

used in this country is that of camellia hedges. I have never felt that these were a great success as seen in places like Porto in Portugal, where they have very massive hedges of various japonicas: alright as a barrier, but showing very few flowers as they are hidden by the leaves.

The exception is at Puke-iti in New Zealand, which I have copied and had some success with here. This is a hedge of 'Donation' which can be clipped almost like a Privet hedge and yet is a mass of good quality flowers almost obscuring the foliage for quite a number of weeks in the spring. It is a very effective addition to that part of the garden, always admired by visitors.

I have learned many lessons over the years as to how and where to plant a camellia. Originally I followed all the instructions in books and planted them either on a north wall or in light shade. They did very well, but I have changed my planting habits since then when I discovered that, in this part of the world anyway, they can be planted in full sun without detriment and with even better flowering potential. This may be because I live in an area of higher rainfall and less sun-hours than say, the eastern counties of Britain. But certainly in north Devon I can plant them in full exposure. What is even more surprising is that, in an area which I have developed in comparatively recent years, where rhododendrons and camellias have been planted together with other trees and shrubs, the camellias have done extremely well. They have bloomed marvellously, with leaves quite untouched by very severe gales whereas very often some of the rhododendron species and hybrids suffered quite severe damage to their leaves.

Another method of growing them which is not much practised, I think, is as they are seen in Spain and Portugal. Here they can be seen in places like Vigo where there are avenues of them as street trees, and I am starting now to grow some of them up on a trunk.

I had never liked 'Drama Girl' because of its large blousey flowers, but grow this up on a stem and you get a very effective small-flowering tree with flowers looking in proportion.

I had always thought of reticulatas as being rather difficult when grown out of doors without protection, but I have found out in recent years that they will grow exceptionally well if grown in full exposure to both sun and wind, and I have small groups of them growing in the teeth of the south-westerly gales which sweep up my valley. They are covered with massive flowers followed by a heavy set of seed every year, and make a very attractive group.

We are indebted to the USA, New Zealand and Australia for all the hybridising that they do, from which we in this country can select the ones that will do well here. Hybridising is of course made easier in these countries as the seed set is so much greater there. On balance I find that those bred in the Southern Hemisphere are likely to do well in my garden.

A lot of the American hybrids have been deliberately infected with virus in order to produce a variegated bloom; the leaves of these plants often show up the virus in an unsightly way. I prefer to feel that my plant is disease free.

A lot of the listed plants in the nursery catalogues in the USA are sports and many of these, such as *C. japonica* 'Betty Sheffield Supreme' and others, are not stable and may easily lose their distinctive markings. I presume that the set of seed is partly determined by the heat of the sun compared with that in our climate. I went to considerable lengths at one stage to get seed to set, to the extent of putting a beehive into the camellia greenhouse in addition to giving some extra heat, but still had very little benefit from it. I have had one or two successes however by enclosing an individual plant in a polythene tent and doing my cross-pollinating inside it. The only one of these that I named was 'Carolyn Snowdon', (*C. reticulata* 'Buddha' × *C. japonica* 'Ville de Nantes'). It is a semi-double flower of a very striking red colour, a large bloom and with reticulata foliage. It received an Award of Merit at the RHS.

I also tried breeding for scent and for this purpose used a small single japonica known as 'My Darling'. I saw this in Los Angeles where it filled the garden with scent but was disregarded by the garden owner because of its size. I used this as the female plant and used the pollen of quite a number of other scented camellias. The best parent proved to be *C. japonica* 'Scentsation' and this produced a nice semi-double peony form with quite good perfume. I have never named or registered this however, but the late Ken Hallstone of Lafayette had it from me.

Of the New Zealand williamsii hybrids, I have always grown Les Jury's, especially liking 'Elsie Jury' and 'Debbie' among many of his which have done well here, as well as Felix Jury's 'Water Lily' and others. A lot of Professor Waterhouse's seedlings such as 'E.G. Waterhouse' raised in Sydney have adapted themselves well to our climate.

Another point of interest that I have discovered over the years is that camellias grown in the USA may have a completely different form of flower to the same plant when grown in the UK. The difference is in the extra number of petals, and particularly petaloids, which occur in this country in flowers which are pure semi-double on the other side of the Atlantic. One example of this is *C. japonica* 'Guilio Nuccio' which shows many petaloids over here and loses all the attraction of the flower in America, or as I have seen it in Portugal, where the bloom shows its clear 'rabbit's ears'.

I imagine that a lot of this is due to the strength of the sun in these countries in the summer months and I am influenced in attributing this to the temperature, as the camellias that I grow in the camellia greenhouse are much more like the American form than the same plant if I grow it out of doors.

I brought back from California a cutting of 'Rosina Sobeck' and grew one plant of it in the greenhouse and one in the open garden. These were from the same cutting originally, and yet the one in the greenhouse has a pure semi-double flower and the one outside is peony-form, both beautiful in their own way but completely distinct.

Another example is 'Ville de Nantes' which, in spite of having been raised in France, I imagine, is a miserable small flower with a twisted centre when grown in this country, and yet is of exhibition quality, as a semi-double flower with a good boss of stamens, at any camellia show in the USA.

I brought back from Los Angeles a cutting of a seedling which was given to me by the raiser provided that I gave it a name. As it was like a Christmas rose and a clean pink single I named it 'Pink Hellebore'. I brought home the very cutting which had the flower on it and propagated it here. I have had it growing in the garden ever since as a rather desirable, absolutely formal, pale pink double flower, in complete contrast to the original, absolutely pure, single flower – and that can only be for climatic reasons. I still have it labelled 'Pink Hellebore' but as there are now some real hellebores in this country which are double I suppose I can get away with it.

As for the use of camellias for garden

design, I have already mentioned the camellia hedge and the use of standards and also as trees, but a particular plant that I saw originally in New Zealand, which I find exceptionally useful, is 'Spring Festival'. I saw this growing each side of a path leading up to a front door. It is entirely fastigiate, quite narrow and of reasonable height with a small formal double pink flower in proportion to its leaves. This plant can be very useful when designing a new small garden.

My camellia house is quite large and I put it up in 1969 after visiting the USA and seeing the quality blooms they produce if the climate is right. The only way I could approach this was by putting up a greenhouse, unheated except in extreme weather, so that there would be protection from the weather. Here I can carry out disbudding to give perfect blooms which should all come to fruition.

There are certain blooms which are quite unsuitable for growing outside such as *C. japonica* 'White Nun', so well-named with its huge pure white flowers, and also *C. japonica* 'Mrs D.W. Davis' which is always damaged outside.

I also like the greenhouse for growing scented plants such as the species *tsai* and a hybrid of *C. lutchuensis*, which I had from Clifford Parks. With his agreement I named it 'Spring Mist' after I sent it up for an award as a scented camellia – it was given an Award of Merit.

I also grow a number of reticulatas here of which my favourites are 'Harold Paige' and 'Mandalay Queen'.

Another camellia that I grow and rather dislike, because of its enormous poorly-shaped flowers, is 'Howard Asper', but I keep it there because of the 'ooh-aah' effect that it has on visitors. It also makes them appreciate all the more the smaller and more

beautiful blooms further on.

Of the camellias I grow in the rest of the garden I find that the more elaborate forms, anemone, peony and double, are best kept in the more formal part of the garden, whereas the single flowers, the williamsii type and other single hybrids look best in the landscape. I am particularly fond of the reticulata hybrid, 'Inspiration', which is an extremely strong grower with a long flowering season often lasting from December to the following April. Another single deep pink with a long flowering season with me is 'Muskoka', whose deep pink single flowers stand out from a distance. It is difficult to pick out other favourites from the open garden, but perhaps I should mention 'Margaret Davis', 'Grand Slam', and 'San Dimas'.

Finally I would like to say that although I do grow a large number of camellias I can not regard myself in any way as a 'camelliolic'. I like camellias for their great variety of form, single through to formal double, for their variation in size from the miniatures, such as the much admired 'Kitty', to the reticulatas, not to mention the species such as *tsai*. How about also their variation in colour, confined I agree to the range of red, pink and white, but what a range? Fortunately I do not at all want a pure yellow camellia any more than I want a blue rose. I do rather enjoy the purple colour which appears on many of the Portuguese cultivars. They attribute this to cold although I am not sure why as the same effect is not produced over here very much. I particularly like 'Augusto Pinto', a sport of 'Mathotiana', with a white border to the petal that contrasts well with the purple colour of the petal itself when this shows its purple shades.

I also enjoy the season in which they bloom, when few other exotic flowers can be seen except possibly the Himalayan magnolia species: here of course I might possibly be classified as a 'magnoliolic'!

I also admire the shiny leaves of the *Camellia japonica* particularly, and this feature fits into the garden scene rather better than the duller leaves of many rhododendrons, particularly the hybrids.

If you want to meet true 'camelliolics' you need to meet members of the camellia societies in the USA, where many of their members will only grow camellias in their gardens or 'yards' and no other plant except possibly a few evergreen azaleas.

Following on this, there is strong competition for the shows and I have seen bushes cut down to almost a skeleton while still in flower to be ready to grow the best flower in the show for the following year.

For real tunnel vision however, I would recommend you to the eminent Colonel Tom Durrant of Rotorua, New Zealand, and he would agree with this description, as he not only just grows camellias, but even goes to the length of only growing reticulata camellias. I have certainly benefited from this as he has sent me many seeds from his splendid garden and practically all my best reticulatas were raised from his seed.

Dr James Smart is a former member of the RHS Rhododendron & Camellia Committee, and owner of Marwood Hill, the celebrated garden near Barnstaple in N Devon

The Species of the Barbatum Alliance

David Chamberlain

With the possible exception of *R. suc-cothii*, the species of this subsection are undoubtedly closely allied. As with several other species complexes of *Rhododendron* there have been difficulties in the delimitation and the typification of the species. This has led to some confusion in the application of the names to cultivated plants. This article provides the background, explaining the significant changes in the circumscription and synonymy as compared with my account published in the *Hymenanthes Monograph* (Chamberlain, 1982) to that included within the most recent *Rhododendron Handbook* (Royal Horticultural Society, 1997).

These species are attractive red-flowered large shrubs or small trees that make a major impact early in the season. They generally have bristles on the leaf stalks, from which the name of the subsection is derived. The best known of these is the essentially Indo-Himalayan *R. barbatum* (see Fig. 1) which is linked to the Bhutanese *R. argipeplum* by a series of intermediates, some of which have in the past been referred to as *R. smithii* or *R. macrosmithii*, and ultimately on to the much less well known *R. erosum* (see Fig. 2)from Tibet. *R. exasperatum* (see Fig. 3) rounds off this alliance, coming from the area where Tibet, NE India and N Burma meet.

This last species, which remains a relatively small but open bush, is clearly distinct from its immediate relatives, in its large, broad leaves and persistent bud scales. While I doubt that many would grow it for its rather puny flowers, the foliage is spectacular with its purplish hews as it flushes. It is a pity that it is quite so tiresome to propagate vegetatively, but in a sheltered site it certainly repays the effort. It will be interesting to see how recent introductions of *R. exasperatum,* from the peregrinations of Kenneth Cox and others, perform in cultivation.

The problems in distinguishing *R. barbatum* from *R. argipeplum* and *R. erosum* partly arise from confusion as to just what the last two species represent. To resolve this we need to go back to their original descriptions. *R. erosum* was first collected by Ludlow & Sherriff around the Chayul Chu in southern Tibet in 1936. So, how do plants in cultivation relate back to these original collections? For many years a plant raised from seed donated by Dr J Cromar Watt of Aberdeen (no. 30) in March of 1937 has been languishing under the name *R. argipeplum* at the Royal Botanic Garden Edinburgh. This is a large multi-stemmed shrub, about 4.5m (15ft) high, but, more significantly, the leaves are relatively broad, with rounded apices, strongly impressed veins and a thin indumentum on the undersides of the leaves. The Edinburgh Accession books state that the seed was from Tibet but, while there is no direct reference to Ludlow & Sherriff, there is a good match between the live material and the herbarium specimens of *R. erosum* that were collected by Ludlow & Sherriff in

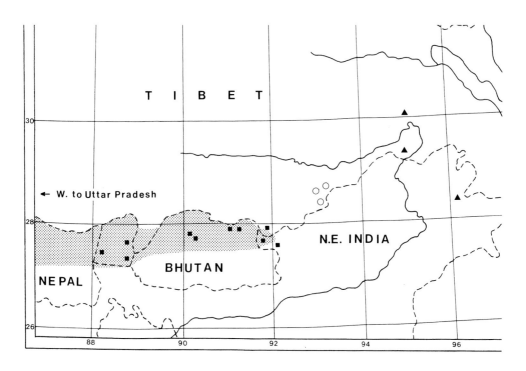

Above: Distribution map of the Rhododendron *Barbatum Alliance*

Key to map*:*

R. barbatum *(grey shading)*   R. argipeplum ■

R. erosum   ○   R. exasperatum ▲

1936. This species has been seen by an Exodus Trek in 1999 on the Bimbi La, above the Tsari Valley in south Tibet.

As there has been a misconception about *R. argipeplum,* we need to redefine its limits by reference back to the original specimens collected by Roland Cooper in Bhutan. While the leaves are broader than is typical in *R. barbatum,* they are significantly narrower than those of *R. erosum;* they have acute to pointed apices, but still have a relatively well-developed leaf indumentum, and their leaf veins are less markedly depressed.

R. smithii Nuttall ex Hook.f. is another name that has been applied within subsection Barbata to plants from Arunachal

Pradesh, just east of Bhutan. In this case our knowledge of the species comes from the type description and plate in the *Botanical Magazine* (Hooker, J D, 1859). This illustration is of a plant from the Lablung Pass, which has strongly convex, narrow leaves, with at least some indumentum. Reference to the Herbarium shows that this falls within the morphological limits of *R. argipeplum.* Incidentally, the name *R. smithii* was earlier applied to a garden hybrid by Sweet. Realising this, Davidian proposed the name *R. macrosmithii* for what is essentially the same entity as Hooker's *R. smithii.*

While I am fairly certain that there is a sharp dividing line between *R. erosum* and *R.*

argipeplum, I am not convinced that the latter can always be distinguished from *R. barbatum*; there certainly is no room for another entity (*R. macrosmithii*) between them. In general the leaves of *R. barbatum* are narrow, with acute apices, no leaf indumentum and not strongly impressed veins. It has a more westerly distribution but almost completely overlaps with that of *R. argipeplum*. In the east of its range *R. barbatum* may have a few bristles in the undersurfaces of the leaves and *R. argipeplum* may have a relatively thin indumentum. It is difficult to ascertain whether this pattern of variation implies a cline from west to east from *R. barbatum* to *R. argipeplum*, or that hybrids are present in the zone of overlap. Despite the potential confusion between these two species, for the vast majority of specimens there is no doubt as to which each belongs. Here, I have to admit that the point at which the differences between two groups of plants are deemed to be sufficient to delimit two species, rather than two varieties or subspecies, is subjective. In other words there may be no 'correct' answer!

The morphological overlap between *R. barbatum* and *R. argipeplum* serves to highlight a general problem in the application of names, where the distinctions between the taxa are not clear cut. It is as well to remember that plants in cultivation may be selected to emphasise the differences implied by the set of names in use. Yet the application of species, subspecies and varietal names should reflect the variation patterns in wild populations; they are not therefore necessarily designed to meet the demands of horticulture.

This is exemplified by the name *R. imberbe,* a name applied to a plant in cultivation from an unknown provenance. As the name implies, the plant concerned lacked the typical 'barbs' or bristles of *R. barbatum*. From the extant herbarium specimens it could well have been a hybrid between *R. arboreum* and *R. barbatum*. In his original description Hutchinson (1928) discounted its possible hybrid origin, comparing it with a wild-collected herbarium specimen from NW India. It is of course entirely possible that this specimen too was hybrid. In any case it seems that the species name *R. imberbe* is not the appropriate name for this plant which may not exist in the wild.

'Barbless' forms of *R. barbatum* do occur naturally and in cultivation and these are sometimes erroneously referred to as *R. imberbe*.

This leads to the conclusion that here are four species in the Barbatum Alliance. To these may be added *R. succothii* to complete subsection Barbata. By way of a summary I hope that the synonymy and short diagnostic descriptions that follow will prove useful.

R. barbatum Wallich ex G. Don

Large shrub or small multi-stemmed tree, 1.5–6m tall. Leaves elliptic to obovate, (9–)11–19 × 3.5–6.5cm, margins plain to moderately concave, apex acute, veins not or only slightly impressed, lower surface generally with a few scattered dendroid hairs and stalked glands, with or without bristles on the main vein; leaf stalks 10–20mm, usually with a dense covering of bristles, occasionally bristles lacking. Flowers 10–20 per truss; calyx 10–15mm, well-developed; corolla 30–35mm, deep red with darker nectar pouches.

R. argipeplum Balf.f. & Cooper (syn. *R. smithii* Nuttall ex Hook.f., *R. macrosmithii* Davidian)

Shrub or small tree, 2–6m tall. Leaves elliptic to obovate, 8–13 × 2.7–4cm, margins moderately to strongly concave, apex acute, veins generally moderately impressed, lower surface with a thin continuous or discontinuous layer of pale brown dendroid hairs that often turn whitish with age, with also with a few bristles on the main vein towards the base; leaf stalks 10–20mm, with a dense covering of gland-tipped bristles. Flowers 10–20 per truss; calyx reddish, 5–10mm; corolla 30–45mm, deep red darker with nectar pouches.

R. erosum Cowan
Shrub or tree, 2.5–6.5m tall. Leaves broadly obovate, 8–10 × 3.7–7cm, margins conspicuously concave, apex rounded, veins strongly impressed, lower surface with a dense covering of hairs at first that becomes thinner with age, also with a few scattered bristles; leaf stalks about 10mm, with a few glandular bristles. Flowers 12–15 per truss; calyx reddish, 3–4mm; corolla 30–35mm, rose-pink to crimson, with nectar pouches.

R. exasperatum Tagg
Shrub or small tree, 2–5m, slow growing; bud scales more or less persistent on the shoots, 11–13.5 × 6–7.5cm, margins moderately concave, veins not or only slightly impressed, lower surface with stout gland-tipped hairs that grade into bristles on the midrib; leaf stalks 5–10mm, with long bristles. Flowers 10–15 per truss; calyx reddish,

4–5mm; corolla brick red with depressed nectar pouches.

R. succothii Davidian syn. *R. nishiokae* Hara)
Shrub or small tree, 1–6m. Leaves oblong to elliptic 5–13.5 × 2.5–5.5cm, apex rounded, minutely apiculate, veins not impressed, lower surface without hairs or bristles; leaf stalks 0–5mm, lacking bristles. Flowers 10–15 per truss; calyx c. 1mm; corolla fleshy, crimson, with conspicuous nectar pouches, 28–35mm.

References
ARGENT, C G C, CHAMBERLAIN, D F COX P A & HARDY, G A (1997). *The Royal Horticultural Society Rhododendron Handbook.*

CHAMBERLAIN, D F (1982). A Revision of Rhododendron II. Subgenus Hymenanthes. *Notes from the Royal Botanic Garden Edinburgh* **39 (2)**; 209–486.

HUTCHINSON J (1928). Plants new or noteworthy. *Gardeners' Chronicle* **83**: 213–14, f.106.

HOOKER, J D (1859). *Rhododendron smithii. Curtis's Botanical Magazine* **85**, t.5120.

Dr David Chamberlain is the author of the *Revision of Rhododendron Subgenus Hymenanthes* for the Royal Botanic Garden Edinburgh, and is a well known authority on rhododendron classification. He is also co-author of *The Genus* Rhododendron *its Classification & Synonymy* and the new *RHS Rhododendron Handbook*

E H Wilson –
The Magnolia Legacy

MAURICE FOSTER

'Stick to the one thing you are after and do not spend time and money wandering about. Probably almost every worthwhile plant in China has now been introduced to Europe.'

Such were Veitch's reported instructions to Ernest Henry Wilson in 1899 when as a 23 year old he was selected to go to China to find and collect seed of the *Davidia* that had been discovered by Augustine Henry some 12 years earlier. The absurdity of Veitch's assumption is evidenced by *Plantae Wilsonianae*, the inventory of Wilson's collections for the Arnold Arboretum in Boston. It comprises probably the richest treasure house of garden-worthy hardy plants collected by any plant hunter before or since. Wilson collected some 3,356 species and varieties of which more than 900 were new, (including 60 rhododendrons) as well as something of the order of 16,000 herbarium specimens. It was an extraordinary record of success and an immense legacy to gardens across the world.

Wilson made four journeys to China, two as a collector for Veitch and two for the Arnold Arboretum. He departed for China for the first time just 100 years ago in 1899. Travelling to America in April to study the latest techniques of plant collection at the Arnold, he went on via San Francisco and Hong Kong to visit Henry in Yunnan. He arrived in October, to confer with the great

man about locating the *Davidia* and to benefit from Henry's first hand experience of Chinese collecting localities and conditions in general. His main collecting areas were in Sichuan and western Hubei, across areas extraordinarily rich in trees and shrubs, including the three great mountains of Emeishan, Wa-shan, and Wa-wu shan. His last visit to China began in early 1910 and he returned to America the following year. His further travels in the East were to take in Japan, Korea and Taiwan.

Wilson introduced nine new magnolia species and varieties from China to our gardens, and his new introductions have had, and indeed are still having, a significant influence on the development of the magnolia as a cultivated plant for cool temperate regions. They have also stimulated much debate among botanists and taxonomists, who have long been defining relationships and drawing specific boundaries between the Wilson magnolias.

Probably the best example of this is **Magnolia sprengeri**. Wilson introduced it into cultivation through his seed lot 688, collected in 1901 on his first Veitch expedition as *Magnolia denudata* var. *purpurascens*. Wilson (*Plantae Wilsonianae*) described the flowers of this collection as '….saucer shaped and vary from rose-red without to rose or pale pink within; the stamens and carpels are also rose-red…a striking object in the woodland landscape.' According to Lord Aberconway (*RHS Ornamental Tree and Shrub Conference 1938*) eight seedlings from this collection were raised by Veitch and sold to Kew, Bodnant and Caerhays at the famous Coombe Wood sale in 1913. Only one, the Caerhays plant, eventually produced superb rosy red flowers. Because of its beauty it was named **Magnolia sprengeri var. diva** – the goddess magnolia (AM 1942). Johnstone (*Asiatic Magnolias in Cultivation*) is lyrical in praise of this tree – 'those who have stood beneath its panoply of hundreds of rosy flowers outlined against a clear blue sky above – a feast not soon forgotten – will surely agree that it is the goddess of that wonderful woodland garden.'

The other Veitch seedlings, although from the same 688 collection, were disappointingly all smaller flowered and white. Dorothy Callaway (*The World of Magnolias*) refers to an unfinished Wilson manuscript in which he wrote that he had packed the 688 seeds in earth and unfortunately mixed them with another magnolia with identical fruit but white flowers – an explanation for the seedling variation.

Wilson refers to the pink form as 'the common magnolia of western Hupeh and eastern Szechuan and is fairly plentiful in moist woods and thickets between 1000 and 1,800m [3,300–5,900ft] altitude' (*Plantae Wilsonianae*). Philip J Savage Jnr (*Newsletter*, American Magnolia Society, **6[2]**, 1969) writes that there were many who took Wilson's comment about the abundance in the wild of the 'Diva' tree with 'a grain of salt' and rehearses the arguments for these doubts. In summary, these are that no-one, including Wilson, seems to have enthused about or even mentioned the wonderful rose-red-flowered Hubei trees until after the Caerhays tree flowered; it does not appear to be figured in Chinese or Japanese literature and evidently was not known in cultivation in either country; all but one of the 688 collection had white flowers and many from the Caerhays tree have since been similarly unexceptional; and the 'fit' with the type described by Pampanini was not good and would better match a Buergeria section plant like *M. cylindrica* or *M. biondii*.

Herbarium material of the type *M. sprengeri* was collected by the Italian botanist P C Silvestri in Hubei in 1912 and described by Pampanini – the flowering specimen was dried and, being precocious, was without leaves and the flower colour was not determinable. Thus according to Wilson's observations, Silvestri's tree was probably pink, supporting the reduction of var. *diva* to the type; if the doubters have their way, it is likely to have been white and var. *diva* the correct designation of the pink form.

What is sure is that the Caerhays tree is unique as the only original representative of the rose pink form in cultivation and, until further work can be done in the field, its taxonomic status as to whether it is the type of *M. sprengeri* will remain in doubt. In any event, it is useful to acknowledge the outstanding horticultural value of the Caerhays tree and recognise the clonal name 'Diva'.

What is also sure is that although some seedlings from this tree and some of its subsequent generations are poor with small flowers and weak colour, many are of the highest horticultural merit. Open pollinated seedling forms, with or without putative hybridity, as well as deliberate crosses, have yielded trees of exceptional beauty and character. The Caerhays tree has turned out to be a most valuable parent, often passing on its sturdy, vigorously branching habit as well as a vivid rose-red or pink flower colour. Its hardiness too has proved an asset and it is being used as a parent in the US to confer hardiness as well as colour. It is reported to have withstood temperatures as low as −18⁰F (−27.7⁰C). Wilson's rose-red single seedling introduction is turning out to be one of the most important of all in generating a whole race of exceptionally fine hardy magnolias.

One of the oldest forms and still worth planting is 'Claret Cup', a Bodnant tree and said to be a direct seedling from 'Diva'. It has 12–14 rosy purple tepals, fading to white inside and was awarded an AM in 1963. 'Copeland Court' (see Fig. 6), raised from Trewithen seed, is a superb rich pink with larger flowers, exceptionally free-flowering on a small tree or large bush. 'Burncoose' is a distinctive rather darker, more purplish form also with larger flowers on a very upright tree. In 'Eric Savill', the colour is an intense reddish purple. The form however is less spectacular with rather crimped and muddled tepals. 'Lanhydrock' also originated from Trewithen seed. It is a sturdy, medium-sized tree with a very distinctive deep, dark reddish pink tone. 'Marwood Spring' is a not dissimilar tree, which originated from seed collected from a seedling of 'Diva' growing in the Porlock garden of Norman Hadden.

All these open-pollinated seedlings have inherited something of the depth, richness and clarity of colour of the original 'Diva'. They mostly arose from trees growing in large magnolia collections and some cross-pollination is likely. All are outstanding garden trees and not particularly demanding in cultivation, in terms of either position or soil, provided it is neutral or acid.

Of the deliberate hybrids, perhaps 'Caerhays Belle' is the best known. As *M. sargentiana* var. *robusta* × *M. sprengeri* 'Diva', it is a cross between Wilson's two most horticulturally influential introductions. It has a definite salmony note which gives its pink a distinctive and appealing tone.

Two outstanding US hybrids from the National Arboretum, Washington with 'Diva' as the pollen parent and *M. liliiflora* the female, are 'Galaxy' (see Fig. 4) and 'Spectrum'. Both are hardy, late enough to escape spring frosts ('Spectrum' is 7–10 days later even than 'Galaxy') with reddish purple and reddish pink flowers respectively, of poise and substance on neat and upright trees of only moderate size but which are genuinely arboreal. Two notable crosses from the well-known American hybridist Dr Frank Galyon are 'Paul Cook' and 'Raspberry Swirl'. The former is a cross with a 'Lennei' seedling and has flowers up to 25cm (10in) across, white with a pink flush; the latter a dark rich reddish purple inherited from *M. liliiflora* 'Nigra'. It has a notably pale interior. From Phil Savage in Michigan, a raiser of some outstanding magnolia hybrids, come crosses with *M. acuminata* as the seed parent: 'Flamingo', said to have foliage resembling 'Diva' and flowers of 'brilliant unfading flamingo pink', and to have survived −29⁰F (−34⁰C) (*Magnolia,* issue 53, 1992); and from the same cross, 'Peachy' with flowers 'orange-red on the outer surface and creamy white on the inner surface, giving the appearance of a mottled peach'. (*Magnolia,* issue 56, 1994). Could this be the harbinger of a new race of 'orange' magnolias? Either as seed or pollen parent 'Diva' will clearly continue to have enormous influence on the development of new garden magnolias.

This is not the case with **M. sprengeri var. elongata** (AM 1955) which with its more compact bushy habit and quite small cream or white flowers seems scarcely to have been used as a parent, and is generally seen only in collections. Wilson collected it as *M. denudata* var. *elongata* and described it as rather rare and pyramidal in habit. Bean (*Trees and Shrubs Hardy in the British Isles*) rates its garden value as equivalent to *M. kobus*, but as Treseder points out, it flowers much later and its impact is thereby reduced.

M. sargentiana and its variety *robusta* also have an uneasy taxonomic relationship. Wilson differentiates the variety 'with its longer and narrow leaves and in the larger fruit'. The type of *M. sargentiana* was described as 'this remarkably distinct species.... grows to a greater size than any other Chinese magnolia and is one of the noblest of its family.' (*Plantae Wilsonianae*). Wilson found a specimen at a hamlet west of Wa-shan, 25m (82ft) tall with a 3m (10ft) girth and a clear trunk for 5m (16½ft). In 1908 he made a special journey to photograph this tree, but it had been cut down. On this visit however, he noted other examples '15–20m [50–70ft] tall...fairly common west of Wa-shan.' He had evidently never seen it in flower.

In a letter to the *Gardener's Chronicle*, 11 June, 1932, James Comber, head gardener at Nymans, states that *M. sargentiana* 'first flowered in England on April 4 1931... at Caerhays, where it was probably planted about 1912, four plants having been obtained from Messrs Chenault and also a seedling from Coombe Wood nursery about that date. In 1911 a young seedling had been planted at Nymans and has attained a height of twenty six feet six inches.' His first-hand description of the flower is detailed; 'the buds open slowly, burst partially and show their rosy purple colouring for some days, and even afterwards the sepals and petals are held together in brush-like form for a few days.... the sepals and petals have varied from 16 to 12 and the number would seem to bear relation to the strength of the shoot carrying the flower.... The outside of the flower is of a rich purple pink and when fully opened measures about eight inches across and shows a delicate mauve-pink interior, which fades gradually to mauve tinted white.'

M. sargentiana (FCC 1935) remains rare in cultivation when compared to **M. sargentiana var. robusta**. This was collected only once, in September 1908, in the type locality on Wa-shan, Sichuan, at 2,300m (7,500ft). Its larger flowers, 20–25cm (8–10in) across, which are more generously produced, are beautifully poised and nodding (FCC 1947) and its tepals do not roll or curl like the type when the flower is fully expanded. The habit of var. *robusta* is a strong multi-stemmed heavily branched spreading tree; the type is taller and less substantial, with thinner and whippier branches. It remains a moot point as to whether the variety warrants separate specific status or whether it falls within the acceptable limits of specific variation of the type. Johnstone gives it specific rank with support from Treseder, the latter on additional grounds that seedlings have never reverted to the type. Spongberg (*Magnolias and Their Allies*) while keeping it as a variety, believes 'it may be best to accord it cultivar status in the future'.

The type species has yielded no named cultivar progeny, nor has it evidently been used for hybridisation. The var. *robusta* on the other hand has produced significant numbers of both forms and hybrids.

A double form grows at Mount Congreve in Ireland and has been named 'Multipetal' by Sir Peter Smithers. It has as many as 19–27 tepals making up rather muddled pink flowers. 'Blood Moon' from the Strybing Arboretum, San Francisco, has the darkest flowers, of a rather striking pinkish purple. There are also beautiful white forms to be found in Cornish gardens. The best known of a number of hybrids with *M.*

campbellii and its subspecies *mollicomata* are 'Hawk', 'Buzzard' and 'Treve Holman' at Chyverton. Probably the richest in colour is 'Philip Tregunna', raised at Caerhays and awarded an FCC in 1992. 'Mossman's Giant' from Oregon has massive foliage and large rather floppy flowers in sargentiana robusta style. 'Arnold Dance' at Burncoose is a large flowered, heavily textured, rich pink cross. 'Michael Rosse' (AM 1968) from Nymans and 'Princess Margaret' (FCC 1973) from Windsor are open-pollinated *M. campbellii* var. *alba* seedlings likely to have *M. sargentiana* var. *robusta* blood. 'Mark Jury' from New Zealand appears to have some var. *robusta* influence.

M. dawsoniana (AM 1939) is a close ally of *M. sargentiana*, differing in its typically multi-stemmed and densely branching habit (see Fig. 5), its glabrous leaf reverse with stronger reticulation and flowers with generally fewer tepals (9–12 as against 12–14). It was collected by Wilson in W Sichuan in October 1908 and again at the same location in 1910. It came to Europe in 1919, sent by Rehder to the Chenault nursery in Orleans like so many Wilson collections. 'The tree is rare and only known from one rather remote locality', Wilson wrote. It is a tree of distinctive personality with its rather dense shrub-like habit and flowers with long lax tepals. These curve outwards and downwards on slender branches in a loose, in some cases floppy, in others elegant, manner and are produced in great abundance. Selected seedlings raised from cultivated plants have deservedly been given clonal names. The colour of these varies from the rich tones of crimson-red in 'Chyverton' (AM 1974) to near white flushed with pale pink in other seedlings. 'Ruby Rose', a Californian seedling has flowers 'darker than normal, 11in [28cm] across when mature' (*Magnolia* issue 37,

1984) and 'Valley Splendour', a form from Windsor, is a showy pink. Perhaps the best form suitable for general planting, from the W B Clarke nursery in San Jose, California, is not surprisingly styled 'Clarke'. This appears to be more compact, not particularly fastidious as to soil or position, flowers at quite a young age, will root from cuttings and has flowers of clear rich pink, paler inside with tepals rather wider than usual and nicely poised on a large upright bush, attaining some 5 × 4m (15 × 12ft) after 14 years from a cutting. Wilson's collections were made at 2,000–2,300m (6,500–7,500ft) altitude and *M. dawsoniana* appears to be perfectly hardy in the UK. Hybrids are few, but both 'Ann Rosse' from Nymans, assumed to be a cross with *M. denudata*, and a Phil Savage hybrid of the same parentage called 'Marj Gossler', have white flowers flushed with pink deepening at the base and are beautifully shaped.

The type of **M. wilsonii** (FCC 1971, AGM 1984) (see Fig. 7) was found in W Sichuan at an altitude of 2,300–2,600m (7,500–8,500ft), on 24 May and again in October 1904 on the second Veitch expedition, under Wilson's number 3137. 'It is quite common in the moist woods and thickets to the south-east of Tachien-Lu, usually in the form of a straggling bush. In late May and early June it is conspicuous with its pure white petals and sepals and bright red stamens and carpels.' His seed batch no. 1374 was collected in the same locality and under this number J C Williams obtained plants from Veitch for Caerhays in 1912. Four years later, Wilson collected what he called *M. nicholsoniana* on Wa-shan at 2,300– 2,800m (7,500–9,200ft) altitude. He noted that it was very rare and confined to this one locality. He also noted the differences as red bark, leaves of a different shape and grey-pubescent below, fewer sepals and petals and a stout peduncle villous along its entire length. Later these differences were regarded as not warranting specific seperation, and it was reduced to a synonym of *M. wilsonii*.

It is entirely appropriate that this magnolia was named to honour Wilson as it is one of the most valuable and beautiful species in the genus. It is easy to grow, it will flower after about five years from seed which germinates freely; it is perfectly hardy and takes less space than most and can be safely pruned to shape. It is said to prefer some shade but in most parts of this country it will grow happily in sun if there is adequate moisture at the root. A large shrub or small multi-stemmed tree, it arches elegantly and displays to perfection its 8–10cm(3–4in) pendant white fragrant flowers with their prominent pink or red carpels. In the best forms these are of a rich crimson-red. Seedlings do vary somewhat in size of flower and depth of colour of the stamens but none have been sufficiently distinctive to become established as cultivars. Hybrids with *M. globosa* and *M. hypoleuca* have been made, but to date to my knowledge none have been named.

Magnolia sinensis (FCC 1931) is endemic to a small area in NW Sichuan. Wilson collected specimens and seed near Wen-ch'uan on his 1908 visit and named it *M. globosa* var. *sinensis*. It has close affinities with both *M. globosa* and *M. wilsonii* but Stapf proposed it as a distinct species in 1923 and most authorities have since recognised it as such. It differs essentially from *M. wilsonii* in its more rounded leaf apex, in the silky hairs covering the juvenile shoots and leaves, and in its light fawn bark. Spongberg concludes that the closest affinities are in fact with *M. sieboldii* and after a detailed comparison of a collection of *M. sieboldii* subsp. *sieboldii* at Martha's Vineyard, Massachu-

setts, with the type collection of *M. globosa* var. *sinensis*, found that the two collections 'could have come from a single gathering'. He thus recognises it as a local and disjunct subspecies of the widely distributed *M. sieboldii*. Horticulturally it seems distinct enough, making a sprawling bush. The flowers are 8–13cm (3–5in) across and rather larger, flatter and possibly more fragrant than either *M. sieboldii* or *M. wilsonii*. It is said to be tolerant of chalky soil. One form of *M. sinensis* has been selected for a cultivar name – 'Ursula Grau'. This form is reported to flower some three weeks ahead of the type. It has 17 tepals and looks something like a semi-double camellia according to Dr Piet van Veen of Ticino, Switzerland. It has a wonderful fragrance and flowers for a second time in August, 'not just a few flowers, but abundant.' (*Magnolia* issue 55, 1994)

Magnolia delavayi (FCC 1913) was discovered in 1866 and introduced by Wilson from S Yunnan in 1899. It was one of his first important finds. It has the largest leaves of any evergreen magnolia, up to 30cm (12in) long and up to 15cm (6in) wide, stiff and parchment-like in texture, a dark sea green in colour, with the young growth on some seedlings a deep purple. The character of the foliage is not matched by the quality of the creamy white flowers which are 15–17.5cm (6–7in) across and sparsely borne. They open at night and fade to a buff-brown within a few hours. Two multipetalled clones are offered by the Louisiana Nursery in the USA. Wilson recorded the species on both sandstone and limestone formations. Treseder refers to its lime tolerance as exemplified by a large specimen at Highdown on the chalk and one at Padstow growing on calcium-rich dune sand.

It is surprisingly hardy for a plant growing at a relatively low altitude in warm temperate Yunnan. However, early specimens were usually planted against a sheltered wall. The great tree at Birr Castle in the comparatively cold midlands of Ireland was no exception. Originally planted in the shelter of the moat wall, it now towers above its protection into full exposure and seems quite unperturbed by the experience. It might thus be worth planting this magnificent evergreen tree more frequently as an open ground plant with suitable wind shelter almost anywhere in the south and allow it to develop more freely to its full majesty. It evidently bears snow well and is less brittle than M. grandiflora. As a young plant it grows freely and several specimens in favoured west country gardens have exceeded 10m (30ft) in height and as much across.

Wilson makes quite frequent reference to **M. officinalis** which he never found in the wild but which was common in cultivation. He introduced it in 1900. The bark and flower buds are valued for medical purposes and Wilson's theory was that the practice of bark stripping had extinguished it in nature.

Ironically, given his subsequent influence on magnolias in horticulture, E H Wilson did not appear to have a particular interest in the *Magnoliaceae*. In his book, *A Naturalist in Western China,* his chapter entitled 'The Flora of Western China' contains no reference to specific magnolias in the text; and allowing for the fact that the book is more an account of his botanical travels than a botanist's detailed field notes, it contains only two passing general references to magnolias and four short mentions of *M. officinalis*, a cultivated species, in 400 pages. Magnolias do not proliferate in the wild and were a very small part of his introductions; harvest time is short and seed is not the easiest to handle and germinate in quantity, and seedlings need some years to mature; and the

majority are not plants for every garden. This may partly explain what appears to be his relative lack of emphasis on what is arguably the world's finest hardy flowering tree. That said, it is fortunate for all who love plants that he largely disregarded Veitch's advice and did his share of 'wandering about'; and that Professor Sargent had the sense to later give him full freedom to do so for the Arnold. His magnolia introductions from China represent a legacy for gardens that is extraordinarily rich; and the influence of the species and varieties he introduced will continue to contribute to the wider planting and appreciation of these magnificent trees.

References

CALLAWAY, D, (1994). *The World of Magnolias.* Timber Press.

COATS, A M, (1969). *The Quest for Plants.* Studio Vista.

HUNT, D, (1998). *Magnolias and their Allies,* IDS/TMS conference proceedings.

HUXLEY, A, & GRIFFITHS, M, (1992). *The New RHS Dictionary of Gardening.* Macmillan

JOHNSTONE, G H, (1955). *Asiatic Magnolias in Cultivation.* Royal Horticultural Society

SARGENT, C S, (1988). *Plantae Wilsonianae.* Timber Press.

MILLAIS, J G, (1927). *Magnolias.* Longmans.

RHS, (1938). Ornamental flowering trees and shrubs conference 1938, *Proceedings of RHS.* Royal Horticultural Society.

TRESEDER, N G, (1978). *Magnolias.* Faber.

WILSON, E H, (1986). *A Naturalist in Western China.* Cadogan Books.

RANKIN, G, (1999). *Magnolias – a Hamlyn Care Manual.* Hamlyn

Checklist of the Cultivated Magnolias, revised edition 1994, The Magnolia Society

Magnolia – journal of The Magnolia Society

Newsletter of the American Magnolia Society

Maurice Foster, a member of the Group and also RHS Floral 'B' Committee, has a fine garden in Kent that includes a large collection of magnolias

Fig. 1: The flowers and leaves of Rhododendron barbatum *at the Royal Botanic Garden Edinburgh (see p.16)*

Fig. 2: Rhododendron erosum *at the RBG Edinburgh (see p.17)*

Fig. 3: R. exasperatum *at the RBG Edinburgh, showing the typical long bristles of the stalk (see p.17)*

Fig. 4: Magnolia *'Galaxy' (*M. liliiflora *'Nigra'* × M. sprengeri *'Diva') (see p.20)*

Fig. 5: M. dawsoniana – *a seedling that illustrates the typically loose, narrow tepalled, drooping flower (see p.22)*

Fig. 6: M. sprengeri *'Copeland Court', a vivid pink seedling of* M. sprengeri *var.* diva *from Trewithen seed (see p.20)*

Fig. 7: M. wilsonii, *a species whose seed germinates freely and flowers in some five years from sowing (see p.22)*

Fig. 8: U Chit Ko Ko, author of the paper on the 1953 Kingdon Ward expedition to the North Burma Triangle (see p.25)

RHODODENDRONS FROM CUTTINGS

Fig. 9 (above left): Pairs of cuttings before and after preparation. Top row – R. fulvum, 'Terracotta', 'Veryan Bay', R. floribundum; middle row – R. viscosum, R. concatenans, R. haematodes, R. wiltonii, 'Tortoiseshell Orange'; bottom row – R. 'Elizabeth Hobbie', 'Temple Bell', R. calostrotum, 'Princess Anne', 'Irene Koster'. Fig. 10 (above right): Cuttings of 'Vintage Rose', R. trichostomum, and 'Olga', showing leaf reduction (see pp. 40 and 41)

Fig. 11: Cuttings growing in modules
(see p.40)

Fig. 12: Cuttings in a mist tent with the side raised
(see p.42)

THE 1953 EXPEDITION TO THE NORTH BURMA TRIANGLE

FOREWORD BY JEAN KINGDON WARD

In 1953 my husband Frank Kingdon Ward and I spent nearly 12 months plant hunting in the 'Triangle' region of North Burma. We were fortunate to have with us two Rangers of the Burma Forest Department – U Tha Hla, and U Chit Ko Ko the author of the paper that follows.

I remember that Frank had been asked by the Burma Government to teach our young colleagues some botany. Clearly Frank's 'lectures' must have fired Chit Ko Ko with genuine enthusiasm for the mountain flora of his native land, and I only wish that Frank could have read this paper by his pupil of some 45 years ago.

Chit Ko Ko was an enthusiastic collector and presser of plants, a great many of which must have been new to him then, coming as he did from a lowland area of Burma. He and Tha Hla worked hard throughout the expedition, often in trying conditions.

I recall one particular day, when we all moved our respective camps on Tagulum Bum a thousand feet higher up the mountain. It was in the middle of May, so already (in those hills) very wet, and there was a relentless south-west gale blowing. Chit Ko Ko, I would guess had never before experienced cold. When we caught up with him on an open hillside at about 2,950m (9,000ft),

Mr and Mrs Frank Kingdon Ward – photograph taken from Return to the Irrawaddy

he was soaked through, shivering uncontrollably, and quite unable to speak coherently, as his teeth were chattering like castanets. Also, his lips were alarmingly blue. He didn't complain, but I think he appreciated having his hands and his back vigorously rubbed, until circulation was restored. The exertion fortunately restored *our* circulation, too.

Our young Burmese colleagues were always most generous in sharing with us specimens of plants we might ourselves have missed, particularly on a subsequent occasion in 1956, during an expedition to Mount Victoria (in central Burma), when Chit Ko Ko was with us again. One night at Mindat, our rear base, we suffered the theft of several bundles of dried herbarium specimens – stolen, presumably, because of the invaluable zip-up blanket bags in which we had hoped to keep our dried plants dry. Neither the bags nor the dried plants were ever recovered, and the loss was serious, for all that it was 'worth' no more than the cost of a lot of apparently useless hay. However, the Herbarium of the British Museum (Natural History) can thank the generosity of Chit Ko Ko and his fellow Forest Ranger for plugging from their own collection, the numerous gaps in ours, caused by this theft. This must have caused them many hours of work, and we were both touched and deeply grateful to them for their kindness. I remember them both with great affection.

By mid June in North Burma the monsoon is considered, officially, to have arrived, and rain falls daily in solid sheets (it had already been falling daily for a month at least, but that apparently did not count). Nevertheless, there is a subtle change in the wetness, in that by June, the spring flowers are all pretty well finished, and for the next three months or more the vegetation lacks interest. That is when the boredom has to be kept at bay (sickness also, with luck, although we did not have an awful lot of luck that rainy season, in that respect) so the first dry days in October were a joy. All of us felt rejuvenated as we prepared for two more highish camps on our chosen mountains, Tagulum Bum and Htama Bum, in order to collect seed of ornamental plants that should be hardy in the gardens of Britain.

During the rains, when one hasn't really enough to do, the day curiously seems about 50 hours long. But during the autumn frenzy of collecting, labelling, drying, dividing and packing seed for about 15 subscribers, the day shrinks to only 12 hours – it must be something to do with relativity! But somehow it all comes right in the end, helped by the indescribable pageant of colour at 3,000m (10,000ft) as one looks down on a forest tapestry of scarlet, gold and every dazzling colour in between, I see that I am writing in the present tense; well, that's how it still feels. Forty years and more ago, but it seems like yesterday.

PLANT HUNTING WITH KINGDON WARD

U CHIT KO KO

Our objective in 1953 was the region known as the Triangle, situated in the Kachin State of the Union of Burma, north of Myitkyina. No serious botanical collecting had ever been done in this area; and though as a result of previous exploration by Mr Frank Kingdon Ward in adjacent areas, it was known what types of vegetation, and what sort of flora would occur there, it required, and still requires, much further work to give a complete picture of North Burma.

The ultimate goal was the group of high peaks forming part of the watershed between the eastern and western branches of the Irrawaddy. It is among these peaks that the Hkerang Hka, a left bank tributary of the Mali Hka (or western branch) rises. The approximate position of the group is 26^0 50'N, 98^0 15'E, the highest peak, called Htama Bum, rising 3,610m (11,845ft) above sea level. I shall refer to them as Arahku peaks.

The Triangle, whose apex is the confluence of the two branches of the Irrawaddy at Tanghpre, 43.51km (27 miles) above Myitkyina and whose ill-defined base lies a little north of the 27th parallel of latitude, is entirely mountainous. In fact, North Burma and north-eastern Assam together make up part of the underbelly of the Sino-Himalayan plateau, which stretches for 3,220km (2,000 miles) across Asia. This underbelly has been so deeply and widely eroded that it no longer bears any outward likeness to a plateau, and has in fact become somewhat detached from the main plateau; and although this isolation is geologically recent (dating only from the beginning of the Pleistocene glaciation), the climatic and other changes, then initiated, have left indelible marks on the flora.

While, therefore, the flora of North Burma in general, and of the Mali Hka–Nmai Hka watershed in particular, could readily be inferred from what was already known of the surrounding areas, there was good reason to think that many new species remained to be discovered, even though the height of the peaks in the Triangle did not warrant belief in an extensive alpine flora. And so it proved.

There would, of course, be less scope for new vegetation types than for new species, since it takes a major climatic change, acting over a long period of time, to bring about the former, whereas new species may result from smaller causes. We established that the north Triangle had been glaciated, which glaciation, lasting through perhaps a million years, must have brought about a fundamental change of vegetation types; but these would not differ appreciably from other vegetation types of North Burma, where the marks of glaciation are even plainer.

Change of climate alone, consequent on the Pleistocene glaciation, is, however, not the only reason for the unusually rich and varied flora of North Burma. The dynamic events of the changeful and intermittent ice age have certainly been a major factor, causing migration, extermination and re-introduction of species. But hardly less important has been the isolation of areas, the compression and telescoping of several phytogeographical regions within a small area, and the immigration of new species. Here differences of altitude have played a major role.

Over large parts of the earth's land surface, the phytogeographical regions are in contact, if at all, in two dimensions only, being separated from one another by deserts, by oceans, or occasionally mountain ranges. In the Triangle, as in many other mountainous areas, they are in contact in three dimensions. It is not necessary to follow up all the implications of this truth here, but it is obvious that whereas the alpine region is the most isolated, the temperate region, between 1,500 and 3,000m (5,000 and 10,000ft) is in close and uninterrupted contact with two distinct phytogeographical regions – Indo-Malaysian below, and alpine Sino Himalayan above. This perhaps accounts for the fact that the temperate zone is the most prolific of all in endemic species.

Journey

In January 1953, myself and U Tha Hla, Silviculturist Ranger, were deputed by the Forest Department for plant collections to assist Mr Frank Kingdon Ward, the famous British botanist and plant hunter, in the above area. On 6 March, after hurried preparations, we left Rangoon by train, travelling to Mandalay, thence to Myitkyina, where the railway ends and the road to China and Tibet begins.

We had brought an assortment of stores, botanical collecting equipment and apparatus from Rangoon, and an old torn tent was kindly lent by Mr D Silva, the Divisional Forest Officer, Myitkyina. We left Myitkyina by jeep on the 8 March, reaching a sub-divisional headquarters called Sumprabum on the 19th. Just before reaching Sumprabum, we collected a rhododendron at about 450m (1,500ft) above sea level, namely *R. simsii* with large bright red blooms. It grows gregariously on the rocky bank of the stream and these shrubs in full bloom presented a very beautiful sight. It is supposed to be the only rhododendron that thrives in the lowest level.

As soon as we arrived at Sumprabum, we met Frank Kingdon Ward who took us up to his bungalow, where his charming wife entertained us with afternoon tea.

The next day we went out with Kingdon Ward, to the neighbouring jungle lying on the west of Sumprabum. We noticed *Styrax, Michelia, Ficus benjamina, Duabanga sonneratioides,* with *Dipterocarpus* and other tropical evergreen rain forest trees common here. The altitude of Sumprabum is 1,207m (3,960ft) above sea level.

Mr and Mrs Kingdon Ward left for Hkinlum, some 85 miles or 10 days march from Sumprabum, on the 21 March. We remained at Sumprabum to complete necessary arrangements and to follow them in a few days.

On the 30 March we started on foot, crossed the Mali Hka at Ningma Daru by a dugout, and in four days reached the Hkang Hka which was crossed by a bamboo raft. Throughout the 10 days journey to Arahku we followed a general north-easterly direction, halting at Arahku for a day's profitable exploration and a visit to the Arahku Silver Mines. We hunted for and collected specimens of *Rhododendron dendricola*, a very graceful rhododendron in flower. On the 12 April we crossed a rickety cane suspension bridge about 30m (100ft) long, just a furlong and a half before reaching Hkinlum. We collected a beautiful sweet-scented white *Styrax* specimen on the way to Hkinlum. We set up our base camp at Hkinlum and were joined by Mr and Mrs Kingdon Ward, so our party was now complete. Though Hkinlum is exactly at the same altitude as Sumprabum, we noticed at once, that certain trees, familiar at the latter place, were not seen here; for example *Ficus benjamina, Michelia montana,*

Duabanga sonneratiodes, Aesculus assamica, Dipterocarpus and *Terminalia myriocarpa.* Several of these, however, became prominent further down the valley of the Hkrong Hka. Their absence at Hkinlum was obviously connected with the proximity to the high peaks. On the other hand, a number of trees not seen at Sumprabum were prominent at Hkinlum; e.g. *Prunus cerasoides, Bucklandia populnea, Manglietia insignis, Myrica nagei, Acer campbellii* and others. It cannot, however, be too strongly stated that, below 1,500m (5,000 ft) the flora of the two areas is essentially the same, any differences being mainly due to minor differences of climate which here means temperature.

Plant Hunting

After exploring the immediate surroundings during the whole of May, the first trip to the alpine mountain was arranged. The first peak to be climbed was Tagulum Bum, 3,512m (11,523ft). Two camps 2,450 and 2,750m (8,000 and 9,000ft) were established. Three weeks were spent in collecting specimens. The weather conditions there were extremely bad in May but the rewards were compensating. Numerous species of *Rhododendron, Magnolia* and other alpine plants were in flower in almost every colour. In June three weeks were spent on another mountain. Htama Bum, 3,617m (11,866ft). A camp at 2,750m (9,000ft) was set up; here too weather conditions were unpleasant. We seldom saw the sun for three weeks, and a thick impenetrable mist shrouded the entire countryside. After June the forests are devoid of any flowers and continue so for the rest of the rainy season.

Kingdon Ward says that the climate of the Triangle does not differ appreciably from that of other comparable parts of North Burma – that is to say, prolonged summer rain, followed by a drier cold weather. The four seasons are well marked, and become more so with the increase of altitude up to about 2,750m (9,000ft). In the alpine zone, however, it is impossible to distinguish more than three seasons.

In 1953, spring in Hkinlum was abnormally wet. This was followed by an unusually dry August, the break in the monsoon lasting about a month with temperatures up to 32°C (90°F) and high humidity. Such August breaks, however, as I recall, are not unusual in North Burma, when little rain falls – and that mostly in the form of short thunder storms, often at night. The fact is that in mountainous North Burma, microclimates within the general framework are common. The most obvious deviation from the familiar monsoon climate of Burma is, of course, the presence of a sub-arctic climate in the north (becoming cold temperate in the Triangle), which affects adjacent areas. Ground frosts occur as low as 1,200m (4,000ft) (as at Hkinlum, where the hillsides have been cleared), while above 3,000m (10,000ft) snow lies deep for three or four months.

The Vegetation Types of the North Triangle

North Burma is almost completely covered with forest. There are three minor – but none the less important – exceptions to this:

(I). *The banks of rivers*. This includes especially the area between low water mark and flood level, and also areas above high flood level which are covered with sand. In the latter the vegetation shows a transition to forest, though the species are often peculiar. This river valley vegetation is, of course, no more than a narrow strip lining either side of the permanent stream bed; but along the many hundreds of miles of rivers, large and

small, it amounts to a considerable area, and the immersible vegetation type includes a surprising number of species.

Four distinct habitats are met with: (a) rocky cliffs, (b) pure sand, (c) continuous stretches of comparatively small water-worn stones with no sand or soil visible between them and (d) piled up boulders.

Silt rarely occurs and where it does locally, it is due to the presence of a small, slow jungle stream. There are, however, gradations between (c) and (d), with occasional (and often temporary) admixtures of silt. Above flood levels, sand is almost always piled up on low shores for a greater or smaller distance; but vertical cliffs, or boulder banks, are followed immediately by thick forest.

Each of the above habitats has its characteristic species, besides species common to more than one habitat. The most interesting plants of this area (i.e. temporary stage on the way to forest) are those which at some period are more or less submerged, especially shrubs. They are gregarious, like *Homonoia riparia*, scattered or in dense mixed thickets where such plants as *Eugenia, Euonymus, Ligustrum, Rosa, Camellia, Rhododendron simsii* and others occur.

The leaves of almost every shrub, annually submerged, are long and narrow, either narrow-lanceolate or linear-lanceolate, and leathery. This is true of all the species mentioned above except *Rosa bracteata* which, with a species of *Phyllanthus* growing under similar conditions, has finely divided leaves. Other examples of narrow-leafed plants are *Ficus pyriformis, Strobilanthes, Salix tetrasperma*, grasses, ferns, and *Cyperaceae*. A much smaller, completely prostrate undershrub is the curious *Rhabdia lycioides* which grows in almost pure sand, usually well below high flood level. Herbaceous plants include a creeping fern (*Goniopteris*) and the *Arum*-like

Cryptcoryne, which forms compact colonies wedged between stones. Most of this strand flora flowers in the winter, at low water, either after the river has begun to fall in October, or in the hot weather of March and April.

From the practical point of view, a knowledge of this river bank sere is imperative for the selection of plants suitable for reclamation work.

(II) *The zone of cultivation*. This extends intermittently from the lower valleys, less than 600m (2,000ft) above sea level, to about 1,830m (6,000ft). Between these limits, much of the country has been cleared of forest and is covered with crops or with secondary growth, undergoing several metamorphoses before its final return to climax forest – which of course it is never permitted to do. Cultivation, however, is confined to south and west slopes; north and east slopes, precipitous rocky slopes, gullies and ravines are untouched. Thus even within the zone of cultivation, in the most thickly populated districts, a good deal of climax forest survives.

Many widespread herbaceous and undershrub plants occur in this zone. Some of these are found in connection with cultivation all over South-East Asia and even further afield; certain *Compositae* and grasses, for example, which are provided with good means of dispersal and quickly seize on unoccupied ground as soon as it becomes available, either through the felling of forest for *taungya* cultivation (shifting cultivation) or the cutting of paths.

Many orchids, too, which will not grow inside the dank forest, are able to establish themselves on solitary trees left standing on cultivated slopes. These, like many other herbaceous plants commonly found on roadside banks where they may grow gregariously, are as much a part of the Indo-Malayan flora as are the forest trees, to which they are accessory. They are not, like weeds of cultivation, intruders, though they may appear to be so, because, in the forest, they are much more scattered. Such Indo-Malayan herbaceous plants include species of *Begonia, Chirita, Impatiens, Viola, Didymocarpus*, many ground orchids, and others.

Some of the most interesting herbaceous plants met with were those which occur in villages, brought in perhaps long ago from outside by the people themselves. Examples are *Iris* sp. (allied *I. watii*) and *Hemerocallis*, neither of which sets seed, and neither of which grows outside the villages, though the iris at least occurs in almost every village. The same is perhaps true of the tea bush (*Camellia sinensis*) in the warmer zone, and of another species of *Camellia*, which might be a substitute for tea in the cooler zone, found only in Hkinlum and adjacent villages.

The presence of these plants is suggestive, and a knowledge of their concurrence and distribution might furnish valuable clues to anyone enquiring into the history of the hill tribes of North Burma. One feels compelled to ask, who brought these plants here? And when and whence? Above all, why?

(III) *The alpine zone on the mountain tops above 3,000m (10,000ft)* This is probably the most extensive non-forested area in North Burma. The alpine vegetation may consist of elfin wood (especially *Rhododendron* species), or of scrub (also largely *Rhododendron*, with *Prunus, Sorbus, Vaccinium*, or of *Arundinaria* with a few scattered undershrubs; all these exclude tree growth.

Where the summits reach 5,200 or 5,500m (17,000 or 18,000ft) there is an extensive zone above the tree line filled with alpines – the real arctic alpine vegetation –

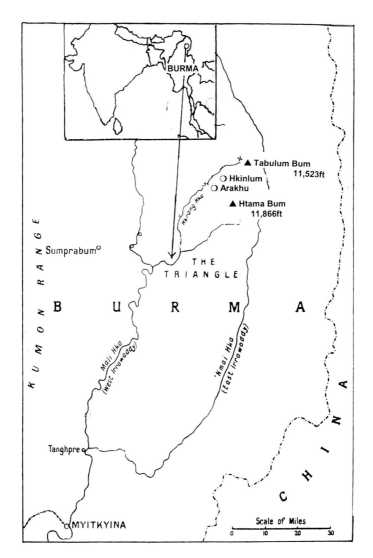

Above: Sketch map of the North Burma Triangle and the area of the 1953 expedition

or, as the limit of plant life is approached, very open with widely scattered herbaceous plants. Even moss and lichens are rare here, and of few species.

At lower altitudes an alpine vegetation clothes the precipitous ridges which lead up to the exposed wind-swept summits. It also descends the steep gullies, which are kept open by running water, and by falling rocks.

In its entire form, about 3,650m (12,000ft) the alpine vegetation consists of turf and sedge, with many scattered and gregarious flowering plants, either of low stature (*Pleurogyne, Lloydia, Cremanthodium, Gentiana, Saxifraga, Viola*) or, forming flat compact mats pressed against the rocks, *Androsace, Arenaria, Rhododendron, Diapensia*, in great variety. This alpine flora is comparable with the European alpine flora, or with the flora of the Arctic; and so also is the vegetation type. It includes a number of endemic genera, *Omphalogramma,*

Cremanthodium, Oreosolen, Nomocharis, besides entire sections of large genera such as *Primula* and *Rhododendron*, sufficient to raise the alpine and sub-alpine region of North Burma to the rank of a phytogeographical region (Sino-Himalaya) in spite of an admixture of arctic and northern forms.

This Sino-Himalaya flora is the most isolated of all the vegetation types of North Burma, and is discontinuous, the mountain top floras being cut off from one another by deep forested valleys.

Type of forest in the north Triangle
The forest cover of North Burma is divided into five main types, of which three are represented in the north Triangle; these are stratified according to altitude. The three types represented are:

(I) *Tropical broad-leaved evergreen forest*, which is a northward extension of the Indo-Malayan phytogeographical region. In the Kachin State this type still persists in the low lying valleys to about 28⁰N: and in the Arahku-Hkimlum area it reaches an extreme altitude of about 1,800m (6,000ft) though it is more characteristic of the river gorges at 900–1,200m (3000–4000ft).

(II) *Temperate broad-leaved rain forest*, which is in part a westward extension of the east Asiatic phytogeographical region, though separated from China by high mountain ranges and deep gorges. Temperate forest covers most of the North Triangle between 1,500 and 2,700m (5,000–9,000ft) and includes a great variety of broad leafed trees, both evergreen and deciduous.

(III) *Silver fir–rhododendron forest*. This, the highest forest belt, is under snow for three months in the year in the Arahku-Hkimlum area, and for six months in the year further north, where the mountains are much higher.

Pine forest is entirely lacking in the north Triangle, where we met with neither a single pine tree, nor any plant of *R. arboreum*.

Mixed Temperate Forest is also wanting; we found neither *Picea, Larix* nor *Tsuga*. In fact, the only gymnosperms we noted, other than *Abies*, were a dwarf juniper and *Taxus*, (both above 3,000m/10,000ft); and two very rare species down in the valley at 1,200–1,500m (4,000–5000ft) – a *Podocarpus*, and an unidentified genus with leaves like a *Metasequoia*. We saw no sign of *Taiwania*.

The three main forest types briefly mentioned above are further divisible on the basis of dominant families or genera, and species frequency, many species having a considerable vertical range, with of course an optimum altitude. Thus the broad belt of tropical evergreen forest which fills the deep valleys and spreads upwards among the foothills, can be subdivided into a lower, narrow tropical belt, and an upper, broader sub-tropical belt, although at intermediate altitudes the distinction between them is necessarily blurred. It is worth noting, however, that a change of forest type is almost always accompanied by a change in the dominant bamboo genus, or species.

Again in the temperate belt, a distinction between the lower warm temperate and the upper cool temperate forest is not difficult to uphold. Thus we may recognise five forest types in the north Triangle, out of the eight described for North Burma in the earlier monograph, written by Kingdon Ward. It will be useful to give a brief account of each, mentioning a few of the more outstanding trees.

(I)Tropical evergreen rain forest
This type is barely represented in the Arahku-Hkinlum area, and need not detain us. Even at 900m (3,000ft) altitude, where

the summers are hot and no frost enters, and with ample atmospheric humidity throughout the year, the effect of the adjacent high peaks is already beginning to make itself felt. A number of trees mentioned in the earlier monograph as characteristic of this zone (e.g. *Terminalia myriocarpa*, *Mesua ferrea*, *Duabanga sonneratiodes*, *Gmelina arborea*, *Dipterocarpus*, *Shorea*, *Spondias*), though occurring lower down the valley, had disappeared before we reached Hkinlum. Nevertheless the forest lining the Hkerang Hka gorge, though composed largely of species not seen at Sumprabum (or even in the valley of the Mali Hka) comes within our conception of tropical forest. Common trees include species of *Elaeocarpus*, *Echinocarpus*, *Styrax*, *Eugenia*, *Manglietia*, *Albizzia*, *Daphniphyllum*, *Prunus*, *Pieris*, and *Ficus* (at least one species) besides several big laurels, *Rubiaceae*, and others.

Though forming only a small proportion of the total forest, this zone is interesting by reason of several rare species, and of importance because of its lining the steep river banks – rivers being the only economic means of transport under present conditions. The rarest tree met with, a single specimen of *Podocarpus*, and the strangest plant, an epiphytic lily of the 'Martagon' type, belong to the borderline between tropical and sub-tropical forest.

(II) Sub-tropical hill jungle

This is well represented in the north Triangle between 1,200 and 1,800m (4,000–6,000ft), above which it passes gradually into a definitely temperate forest type. It lies entirely within the zone of cultivation, and on south and west slopes is represented mainly by second growth, which, however, may include woodland of 20 or more years standing (such woodland is set aside for furnishing building poles). By far the most interesting tree is a tall gymnospermum whose identity, in the absence of flowers or fruit, we were unable to determine; though microscopic examination of the wood is likely to furnish a clue. It is an extremely rare species, at least as a fully grown tree. Common are species of *Diospyros*, *Rhus*, *Schima*, *Elaeocarpus*, *Terminalia*, *Styrax*, *Zanthoxylum*, also *Altingia excelsa*, *Erythrina indica*, *Alnus nepalensis*, *Bucklandia populnea*. Less common are *Helicia*, *Ternstroemia*, *Eriobotrya* and *Sterculia* (a small tree with reddish flowers like *S. coccinea*).

The majority of the species in the sub-tropical belt belong to a few families only, notably the *Fagaceae* (*Quercus*, *Castanea*, *Castanopsis*), *Rutaceae*, *Magnoliaceae*, *Theaceae*, *Rubiaceae*, *Lauraceae*, and *Moraceae* (*Morus laevigata*, *Ficus*), together with the genera mentioned above.

Climbing plants abound in this warm damp climate, and include species of *Clematis*, *Lonicera*, *Jasminum*, *Smilax*, *Vitis*, several *Asclepiadaceae* and *Apocynaceae*. Frequent scramblers are *Toddalia aculeata* and *Aspidopterys* species.

Characteristic and abundant is the epiphytic flora, including many *Orchidaceae* and ferns, *Ericaceae* (*Rhododendron dendricola*), *Vaccinium*, *Agapetes*, *Pentapterygium*, *Asclepiadaceae*, *Hedychium* species, and so forth.

The composition of the hill jungle, however, varies considerably with its distance from the high peaks. Nearer the peaks the more tropical families rapidly decrease, while the more temperate families increase in numbers and variety.

There are many useful and possibly valuable timbers, but no species forms pure stands, and extraction, except perhaps close to the larger streams, is a major problem.

(III) Warm-temperate rain forest 1,500–2,100m (5,000–7,000ft): cool-temperate rain forest 2,100–2,700m (7000–9000ft)

In the north Triangle this type agrees fairly closely with the description given in the earlier monograph; the differences noted are mainly those of composition, a number of new species being added, while many of those mentioned as characteristic (e.g. *Decaisnea, Dobinea, Pottingeria*) were not met with in the Arahku-Hkinlum area.

Perhaps the most striking trees of the warm temperate belts are *Gordonia axillaris* with flowers 15cm (6in) in diameter, *Rhodoleia forrestii, Helicia excelsa* and several species of *Rhododendron*, including *R. stenaulum,* (syn. *R. moulmainense*) *R. genestierianum* and a maddenii ciliicalyx species. Oaks, laurels and *Magnoliaceae* abound; also a species of *Calamus* which ascends to nearly 2,100m (7,000ft). The epiphytic flora, which includes several shrubs – notably *Agapetes* – is varied, but climbing plants, lacking the summer heat they need, are on the down grade.

There are a few deciduous trees, but not enough to colour the autumn forest. On the other hand, several autumn-flowering trees are sufficiently abundant to brighten the slopes in November.

Several of the trees mentioned serve to indicate the upper limit of the warm temperate zone, but the dividing line must never be regarded as fixed; on the contrary, the number of genera with species in several zones ranging sometimes through 1,800m (6,000ft), is a measure not only of its fluidity, but also of the fierce continuous struggle which goes on always between the floras of two superimposed phytogeographical regions to extend their boundaries.

This is apparent, not only regarding familiar genera such as *Ilex, Castanopsis, Quercus, Rhododendron* and *Acer* 1,200–2,700m (4,000–9,000ft), but equally among others less familiar such as *Eriobotrya,* 1,200–2,100m (4,000–7,000ft); *Helicia,* 1,050–2,000m (3,500–6,500ft); *Styrax* (four or five species), 1,050–2,400m (3,500–8,000ft); *Pieris,* 1,050–2,900m (3,500ft–9,500ft); *Schima,* 1,200–2,600m (4,000–8,500ft) and *Symplocos,* 1,050–2,900m (3,500–9,500ft); *Bucklandia populnea,* to mention but one species, has a vertical range of over 1,200m (4,000ft) in the Arakhu-Hkinlum area. This mutual pressure is exerted by one phytogeographical region on another, not only laterally where these adjoin, but also vertically in the mountains.

The next zone, the cool temperate forest, in latitude 27°N is in some respects equivalent to the forests of lower altitudes in much higher latitudes – perhaps to those of the moister parts of western Europe. Its composition is, however, partly eastern Asiatic. Here autumn colour becomes a major feature, indeed the forests flush with colour twice a year, in spring, when the magnolias, rhododendrons and cherries come into blossom and the breaking leaf buds add a rich mosaic of greens, yellows, purples and reds; and again in autumn when the dying year flings a patchwork of scarlet and gold over the hillside.

Among the most brilliant trees at this season may be counted *Sorbus, Acer, Viburnum, Gamblea, Enkianthus* and *Pyrus.* During the height of the rains, however, and in the depth of winter, the temperate forest is sombre indeed; for even at 2,400–3,000m (8,000–10,000ft) it is largely evergreen, with rhododendrons, *Ilex, Symplocos,* oaks, some laurels and *Magnoliaceae* retaining their leaves; while other trees (*Eriobotrya* sp.) are naked only for a very short time.

This is the zone of the big-leaved tree rhododendrons, of *R. sinogrande* and others, one of which, with glorious yellow flowers, as outstanding in May (we did not see any of the others in bloom). The big-leaved species (Grandia and Falconera sections) at 2,700m (9,000ft) tend to form almost pure rhododendron forest; and though their trunks are gnarled and twisted to an extraordinary degree, they are large enough and abundant enough to provide an unlimited supply of timber for special purposes. The wood is extremely hard and close-grained, and takes a good polish. It would be invaluable for veneer and panelling. These trees seem to be immortal; I estimated many of them to be over 200 years old, and rarely did we see a dead rhododendron.

There is also a great variety of shrub rhododendrons, including a number of epiphytic species. In fact, in the cool-temperate forest *Rhododendron* and *Magnolia* are dominant genera, so much so that it might properly be defined as the zone of *Magnoliaceae* and *Ericaceae*.

Notable trees are *Magnolia rostrata, M. campbellii (mollicomata), Ilex nothofagifolia, I. sikkimense, Acer wardii, A. sikkimensis*, and species of *Tetracentron, Zanthoxylum, Michelia, Eriobotrya, Schima, Betula, Styrax, Illicium*, several large *Araliaceae* and *Fagaceae (Quercus lamellosa* and *Q. pachyphlla)*.

The species of *Primula petiolares* and a Candelabra species likewise belong to this zone, together with species of *Begonia*, several ground orchids and a few *Compositae*.

A noted feature is the swathing of the big trees with moss, which not only packs the trunks, but hangs in long festoons from the limbs. In this moss numerous perennial epiphytes, both woody and herbaceous, spring up from seed; in fact, there is hardly a tree in the forest which cannot start this way. Many continue as epiphytic all their lives, and when fully grown are often connected with the earth as well by means of a great root which has grown down the side of the trunk until it reaches the ground (e.g. *Sorbus*). The thin-barked rhododendrons, however, carry no moss.

(IV) Rhododendron–silver fir forest

The Burmese and probably Chinese, silver fir is found on sheltered slopes as low as 2,700m (9,000ft) in the North Triangle, as high as 3,600m (12,000ft) in North Burma generally. Though it forms practically pure stands, the trees are rather far apart, the intervening space being filled with *Arundinaria* and *R. arizelum* – one of the big-leaved trees, and to a lesser extent with another tree rhododendron species of the Thomsonia subsection (possibly *R. eclecteum*). In an earlier monograph I referred the Burmese silver fir to *Abies fargesii*; but whether the north Triangle tree is this species or not remains to be seen.

A number of broad-leaved, mostly deciduous trees is associated with the silver fir, notably *Gamblea, Clethra delavayi*(?), *Pyrus*, and species of *Rhododendron* and *Gaultheria*. It may be remarked that *Abies* is practically confined, at this altitude, to the more sheltered slopes, being unable to withstand bright sunshine. Hence, in this zone we find three distinct plant associations: (i) sheltered slopes covered with *Abies–Rhododendron* forest; (ii) exposed slopes with *Rhododendron* – broad-leaved deciduous trees, mostly of small size; and (iii) ridges, which being exposed to both wind and sun, are covered mainly with mixed shrub growth of low stature, including many species of rhododendron (*R. tephropeplum, R. telopeum, R. trichocladum, R. polyandrum* and others) mixed with *Euonymus, Enkianthus, Symplocos, Viburnum, Gaultheria, Vaccinium glauco-album, Taxus* and many other species. All three associations have *Arundinaria* as a fill-in.

Another point of interest is that *Abies*, the only tree other than *Rhododendron* to form pure stands, is local in its occurrence. Thus, while it was a dominant on Tama Bum at 3,000–3,300m (10,000–11,000ft) we did not come across a single tree on Tagulum Bum, only a few miles to the north and very little less in altitude. One gets the impression that though a tough-looking tree, it is in reality sensitive to slight differences in climate.

There was no sub-alpine meadow association within this zone (or indeed, anywhere else), such as is typical of the higher ranges along the China-Tibet frontier. The nearest approach to this was in the steep sheltered gullies, which, being drained dry in their upper parts by October, carried only a limited variety of coarse herbaceous plants, forming nevertheless a type of sere. The more outstanding plants in these gullies are *Caltha, Cimicifuga, Nomocharis, Polygonum, Luzula, Pedicularis, Rodgersia, Astilbe* and several *Compositae* with large leaves.

Seed Collection

At the close of the rains by the end of September, collection of seeds of the trees and flowers marked during the earlier trip as worth growing in the British Isles and temperate European countries began. This was the busiest season of the expedition and did not end till late in October. We had to scale

---

The climax formations of North Burma according to three Primary Divisions of the vegetation on the basis of vegetative type dominant within their respective limits

Forest

Primary divisions –

(1) Forest	150–3,600m (500–12,000ft)
(2) Scrub	3,300–3,900m (11,000–13,000ft)
(3) Undershrub and herbaceous	3,600–4,600m (12,000–15,000ft)

The climax formations –

Tropical evergreen rain forest	150–760m (500–2,500ft)
Sub-tropical hill jungle	450–1,350m (1,500–4,500ft)
Sub-tropical pine forest	450–1,950m (1,500–6,500ft)
Temperate rain forest	1,500–2,400m (5,000–8,000ft)
(a) Warm temperate rain forest	1,500–2,100m (5,000–7,000ft)
(b) Cool temperate rain forest	1,950–2,400m (6,500–8,000ft)
(c) Temperate pine forest	1,350–2,400m (4,500–8,000ft)
Mixed temperate forest	2,100–2,700m (7,000–9,000ft)
(a) Mixed forest	2,700m (9,000ft)
(b) Bamboo forest	2,700m (9,000ft)
Silver fir forest	2,700–3,600m (9,000–12,000ft)

Scrub

Silver alpine rhododendron scrub	3,300–3,900m (11,000–13,000ft)

Under Scrub/Herbs

Alpine turf and scree	3,600-3,600m (12,000–15,000ft)

both the peaks surveyed earlier in the year to collect seeds, particularly those of *Rhododendron*. Seeds of other alpine plants which grew at heights over 3,000m (10,000ft) were also taken. Some plants had to be dug up, especially specimens of primulas. The expedition collected botanical specimens and seeds of 1,500 different species, some of them absolutely unknown, and new to science.

The many hardships that we had to face during the expedition were well rewarded. At times we had to cut a track up the slippery mountain slopes. At one slope six porters laboured for days before a fairly safe path could be hewn out of the mountain side. Bridges had to be slung over mountain torrents. These were made of cane twisted together and tied to trees on either side of the stream. Coming down the steep slopes was far more dangerous than climbing up. One of the greatest difficulties that we had to face was the interminable rain. We found the torture by gnats, mosquitoes, flies, leeches and other insects, and subjection to violent conditions of weather and privation, most trying. Yet, the expedition had been well worth it and we gained a lot from it. We had the opportunity of studying the European vegetation right in our own country and on the summit which we climbed, we had the satisfaction and joy of seeing the orderly growth of plants and vegetation, well kept and tended by Nature, 'The Great Gardener'.

End of Expedition

After many days of plant hunting in the Triangle, we arrived at Suprabum during the second week of December and we were received very warmly by Mr L Sam Naw, Assistant Resident and his staff. Taking a look towards the north east, we saw Htama Bum remaining behind majestically under an azure sky.

References

KINGDON WARD, F, (1945) A Sketch of the Botany and Geography of North Burma, Part I–IV. Reprint from the *Journal of the Bombay Natural History Society* **Vol. 45,** No. 2, April 1945.

KINGDON WARD, F. *Burma's Icy Mountains.* Jonathan Cape & Co, London

MACQUEEN, DR J, (1952). *The Journey and Plant Introductions of George Forrest.* Oxford University Press, Oxford.

U Chit Ko Ko. At the time of the 1953 expedition he was Curator of the Herbarium of the Forest Department in Rangoon. Subsequently he joined the Agricultural and Rural Development Corporation and retired in 1983. Since then he has written, in Burmese, two books, *Saramayri Traveller* (1983) and *The Flower Hunter from Hkaw-Nu-Sone* (1991), receiving a literary award for the latter

The Propagation of Rhododendrons from Cuttings

E G Millais

The conditions under which rhododendron cuttings are propagated vary enormously, and can progress through various stages of sophistication from a simple box covered with either glass or polythene up to the temperature controlled mist systems which are used commercially.

There are basically two main methods of rooting cuttings. One is dependent on keeping the cuttings in an airtight environment, so that the moisture from the compost produces 100 per cent humidity around the cuttings. This can be achieved either by covering a box with polythene, or using one of the deep sided trays with polystyrene covers, which are obtainable from garden centres for between £4 and £12.

A more advanced form of this type of propagator is the purpose built mini-propagator, fitted with an electric heating cable controlled by a thermostat, which will cost anything between £40 to £100 according to size. This method of propagation is very dependent on a high humidity being present at all times, and if the cuttings are showing any stress, the foliage should be sprayed daily with an ordinary hand sprayer.

The second method is the use of mist propagation. All the humidity is supplied by the mist, which is controlled by an artificial 'leaf'. This contains two electrodes.

Normally a film of water connects these, and no mist is supplied, but when this film evaporates, which will correspond to water evaporating from the cuttings, the mist will come on until the film of water connecting the two electrodes is re-established. There is no doubt that this method, which is relatively expensive (£200–£300 for a small unit), will root difficult cuttings much more easily, and it could well be worth the cost for large private gardens as well as some municipal and National Trust gardens.

Success or failure depends very much on the type of compost used. It is essential that this is free draining, has a high percentage of air spaces, and does not collapse on itself while the cuttings are being struck, which can sometimes take almost a year for very difficult varieties.

We find that two parts medium grade peat, which contains about 30 per cent of 1 to 2cm spherical nodules of hard peat to be most satisfactory. This is mixed with one part of a fairly coarse form of composted bark, e.g. Cambark 100. The effect of the nodules coming into contact with the flat pieces of bark ensures plenty of air cavities and perfect drainage. Owing to the texture of the two ingredients it is quite impossible for the mixture to collapse for at least a year. Finally 50g (2oz) of slow-release fertiliser is added for each 100 litres of compost.

This may seem a very coarse mixture to many people, but we find that cuttings in it do not rot away as so often happens using Vermiculite, Perlite and coarse sand mixtures. In time these collapse and often become waterlogged.

Containers should be reasonably large, not less than about 36×23×8cm (14×9×3in), as smaller sizes are subject to an uneven bottom heat distribution. Those with lattice bottoms are ideal as the drainage is so good. However boxes with holes connected by channels are quite in order.

Bottom heat can be supplied by electric cables controlled by a thermostat at between 17–21°C (63–70°F). This is the easiest method for propagating on a small scale. Larger scale operations will probably use small bore heating pipes, circulating hot water from a boiler.

Boxes of cuttings are placed directly over the heating cables, which are covered with 5cm (2in) of sharp sand, and a soil thermometer is used to adjust the thermostat to provide the correct temperature.

If soil warming cables are not available, the ideal temperatures are often reached during the summer months anyway, and cuttings can be struck quite successfully without them. However, as the containers will cool down at night, they will not reach the correct temperature until mid morning, so the cuttings will take longer to root.

Early cuttings

The earliest cuttings to be taken during the year are usually the deciduous azaleas. Some previous literature on rooting azalea cuttings suggested that plants should be forced into growth to provide early cuttings, which will not survive the following winter unless they themselves have made some further growth.

This is not necessary. Cuttings can be taken from forced plants as early as April or from open ground plants as late as July providing the 'wood' is at the right stage of development. Growth before winter is not necessary, but beneficial.

Take cuttings from shoots which are slightly less than half ripe. It will surprise many people that the thicker and more gross the cuttings are the better. Small cuttings are often harder to root and make poor plants. We put all material for rhododendron and azalea cuttings into polythene bags. These are then lightly misted before being placed in a refrigerator for between 24 and 48 hours before striking the cuttings. This definitely seems to increase their capacity to root.

When making cuttings of deciduous azaleas remove the tip and up to 5 or 6cm (2in) of very soft growth. Then remove the heel end to leave a cutting of between 6–10cm (2½–4in) long. This should leave the cutting with approximately three or four leaves (see Fig. 9). Cut across each leaf leaving between a half and a third of the leaf. This leaves the cutting with the maximum amount of foliage that can be supported by the moisture drawn up through the stem of the unrooted cutting (see Fig. 10). If the leaves collapse not enough foliage has been removed, or the humidity is too low.

Some very soft cuttings may collapse anyway, but if these have not recovered and become turgid, within 48 hours, remove more foliage or increase the humidity. However, it could be that they have been taken too early, in which case, wait a week and try again. This problem of collapsing cuttings is more likely to arise in systems without mist, which will benefit from spraying the foliage once or twice a day to begin with.

Deciduous azalea cuttings are not normally wounded. It is, however, essential that the bottom 1cm (½ in) of the cutting is treated with a hormone to encourage rooting. Commercial growers use different strengths of Seradix, which contains 4 indol-3yl-butyric acid, but most unfortunately this is not available to the general public. Amateur propagators can use a form of rooting powder containing 1-naphthylacetin. Garden centres usually supply small containers of this, such as Murphys and Strike. They are only available in one strength, and this must be used for all types of cutting. This is a most unsatisfactory position, and I can only suggest that if you are aware that a certain type of cutting is difficult to root, try re-dipping the cutting about three weeks after the first insertion. This is only a suggestion, as I have not tried it myself. Dibble cuttings into the compost, as sticking them in directly will remove most of the rooting hormone.

Midsummer cuttings

The next batch of cuttings, most of which will reach the half ripe stage during late June and July, comprise the species rhododendrons, and evergreen azalea hybrids. Once rooted, it is sometimes a problem to remove the smaller cuttings, like *R. primuliflorum, R. trichostomum. R. fastigiatum, R. orthocladum* and the dwarf hybrids, from the compost without damaging the roots. For this reason root the cuttings individually into module trays which contain between 50 and 100 cells, usually measuring about 3.5 × 3.5cm (1½ × 1½ in). This ensures that there is absolutely no root damage when they are potted on the following spring.

The compost used for deciduous azaleas and larger rhododendrons is quite unsuitable for use in module trays as it too coarse to fit into the cells. For this reason use a compost of two parts peat (medium grade passed through a 1cm/½in sieve) and one part (fine

grade) bark. Normal slow-release fertiliser will not mix sufficiently well with the compost to ensure an even distribution into each cell so water lightly with a solution of either phostrogen or Miracid once a month. Discontinue during the winter.

Module trays (see Fig. 11) are very suitable for evergreen azaleas. Cuttings usually become available during July, and most of them will root quite happily without any hormone rooting powder, though its use does hurry things up. No wounding is necessary, and do not remove the tips of the cuttings, but in the case of very strong growing varieties, cut away surplus foliage. No wounding is necessary either on very thin stemmed rhododendrons like *R. primuliflorum, R. trichostomum* and *R. orthocladum*, but those which are slightly thicker, like *R. fastigiatum, R. calostrotum* and hybrids such as 'Wee Bee' and 'Curlew', will benefit by being wounded very slightly.

Other rhododendrons which can be rooted in module trays include those from *R. cinnabarinum, R. heliolepis* and *R. neriiflorum*. Wound these rather thin-stemmed species only lightly, and reduce the leaves to three or four. Cut away about one third of each leaf.

Cuttings of the larger species rhododendrons, which are often available in July, include those from subsections Irrorata, Maddenia, Maculata, Pontica; also *R. fulgens, R. wiltonii, R. flinckii* and the most recently introduced species such as *R. huianum, R. ochraceum* and *R. denudatum*. The early dwarf hybrids, like 'Scarlet Wonder' and 'Red Carpet', are usually ripe at this time, and for these, like the hybrids which follow, make cuttings between 5–10cm (2–4in) long, according to the size of the cultivar.

Do not remove the tip unless it has started to form a flower bud for the following

Fig. 13: Wentworth Castle Gardens. Lady Augusta Walk , looking east from the Secret Garden – large trees to the plan by Humphrey Repton (see p.43)

Fig. 14: Rhododendron *'Queen of Hearts'* (R. meddianum × *'Moser's Maroon')* *exhibited by Exbury at the 1999 Main Rhododendron Competition (see p.73)*

Fig. 15: Camellias as Ikebana exhibited at the International Camellia Congress in Myazaki, Japan (see p.48)

Fig. 16: ICS Congress Japan – R. yakushimanum *on Mt Miyanoura (1,935m), Yakushima Island (see p.50)*

Fig. 17: Camellia amplexicaule, *exhibited at the Flower Show at Agurikaracha Park, Edo (see p.50)*

Fig. 18: Flowers of The High Beeches M. sargentiana *var.* robusta *(see p.53)*

Fig. 19: The 'reborn' M. sargentiana *var.* robusta *flowering at The High Beeches in 1999 (see p.53)*

Fig. 20: Members of the Wessex Branch assembled for planting at Ramster with (right) Miranda Gunn (see p.56)

Fig. 21: The pond area of the garden at Ramster (see p.55)

year. Remove all except 3 or 4 leaves, and leave them on one side of the cutting. Then cut away between a third to a half of each remaining leaf. The cutting is then wounded at its base on the same side as its remaining leaves. The wound should be between 1.5–2cm (1/4–1/2in) long, removing the bark, and cutting into the cambium layer. Those which have indumentum on their stems, like *R. smirnowii, R. bureavii* and *R. yakushimanum* should have this removed so that the rooting hormone has unimpeded access to the cuttings.

The amount of foliage which is cut away in preparing cuttings, which I have described, and illustrated (see fig. 9), suits our method of propagation, and is used extensively by American rhododendron nurseries. However it has to be said that nurseries in France, Holland and Belgium leave on considerably more foliage with, apparently, good results. This is fine as long as the foliage in a box of cuttings does not become too crowded, as this can lead to disease. Foliage which is completely shaded will not benefit the cuttings as no photosynthesis can take place. Make sure the trays of cuttings are placed so that the cuttings face the light.

Late summer cuttings
During late July and August cuttings of some of the larger hybrids and also the yakushimanum hybrids, should be ready. The first of these are usually hybrids of *R. dichroanthum*, such as 'Olga' and 'Terracotta', all the Tortoiseshells, 'Papaya Punch' and 'Apricot Fantasy'. These all root quite easily. Some of the yakushimanum hybrids are more difficult, and will take longer to root.

Cuttings from old hardy hybrids used to be taken in late September or October, but it is now more usual to take them much earlier if they are ready, rather than letting them get too hard. Rooting can take some time, and may not be complete until March or April the following year, and regrettably some may not root at all, using 1-naphthylacetic acid.

Large trays, filled with the deciduous azalea mixture, are probably best for these cuttings, as the drainage remains excellent throughout the winter, but trays consisting of large module cells could also be used, and these certainly help when it comes to transplanting in the spring.

Winter cuttings
There remains one other time for rooting cuttings, which suits some varieties but not others. This is mid-January, and clones as divergent as 'Dr Albert Schweitzer', 'Fairylight' and *R. ponticum* 'Silver Edge' will root easily then. So if you have missed the boat earlier, it might well be worth your while trying again at this time.

The dates which I have given for taking the various types of cutting will vary considerably. Cuttings taken in Cornwall for instance, may well be ready a fortnight earlier than I have mentioned, and those taken in some parts of Scotland may be a fortnight later. On top of this, there is the yearly variation caused by the weather.

Growing on
Cuttings do best in rather subdued light and the amount given to them is important, particularly if they are in a glasshouse where, without shading, temperatures can reach over 30°C (86°F). We find that besides normal greenhouse shading it is necessary to have a layer of opaque polythene sheeting inside the propagating house as additional shading. In addition, in the height of summer, a further layer of opaque polythene covers the cuttings in the form of a tunnel over each benchful of cuttings. In early autumn

this is replaced with clear polythene, as soon as light levels start to fall. (See fig. 12)

These tunnels are particularly necessary if cuttings are being struck under mist. The extra humidity which is produced under them will cut down the amount of water produced through the mist system, and as a result, avoids an overwet compost.

Do not keep the mist going right through the winter. During October gradually reduce it to about two bursts a day, and during mid winter it should be possible to do without it altogether. Too much water during autumn and winter will often produce rather yellow leaves and this can be put right by giving foliar feeds of either Miracid or Phostrogen.

If mini propagators are used, place them where there is an adequate but subdued light. Never subject them to direct sunlight.

Similarly, do not keep on bottom heat right through the winter. High temperatures and no growth do not go well together, and cuttings will tend to rot off unless the temperatures during the winter are reduced. If the cuttings are rooted, or even half rooted, reduce the temperature to 13°C (55°F) in October. Reduce the temperature in November even if the remaining cuttings have not rooted.

Essential tips
Half the battle in rooting cuttings is won or lost in choosing the material for the cuttings. It cannot be over emphasised that cuttings taken from young plants, or at least plants growing strongly, will always root much more easily than those taken from older plants. One of the reasons why Ghent azaleas have the reputation for being difficult to propagate is that nearly all the plants in collections are over 50 years old, with the branches often covered with lichen. Cuttings from this type of plant will hardly ever root.

If cuttings are required, cut down plants in March to about 45cm (18in) from the ground and fertilise fairly heavily. Good cuttings should be available within two years. I have a 50-year-old *R.* 'Gomer Waterer' in my garden which gives a wonderful display every year, but in spite of it still growing about 7.5cm (3in) yearly, I find cuttings from it very difficult to root, compared with those taken from plants between four and five years old.

The position on the plant from which cuttings are taken is important, and very often cuttings taken from a position in full sun will not root as well as those taken from a shady position or the north side of a plant. Some rhododendrons make quite a lot of second growth. If this has firmed up only reasonably well, it does provide particularly good cuttings, which will root comparatively easily.

There are some rhododendrons which are definitely difficult to root, particularly if only 1-naphthylacetic acid is available. These include subsection Fortunea and I have never had much success with *R. makinoi* or *R. insigne*. Some large-leaved rhododendrons like *R. arizelum* and *R. sidereum* will root if very soft new growth is used, particularly if from very young plants.

Rooting cuttings can be very baffling and success one year may not be followed by success the following year, even though exactly the same conditions seemed to be present. Always keep a record of the treatment and timing of each set of cuttings, and even if you are not successful one year, your record may guide you to a success in a later attempt.

E G Millais is a member of the Group and owner of Millais Nurseries in Surrey. He has been on several expeditions to the Sino-Himalaya region

THE RESTORATION OF
WENTWORTH CASTLE GARDENS

DEREK ROGERS

I came to Wentworth Castle Gardens in 1978 with a brief to rehabilitate the derelict 16 ha (40 acre) historical gardens. With the aid of a copy of the original 1713 plans and a large Manpower Services Commission (MSC) workforce we began by clearing the impenetrable formal gardens of the thickets of self-sown sycamore, holly, *Rhododendron ponticum* etc. and restoring the lawns, avenues and drives. These clearances created large empty glades, well sheltered by ancient trees and old hardy rhododendron hybrids, ideal for the introduction of modern hybrid and species rhododendrons, hybrid and species magnolia, camellia and many other ericaceous genera.

Wentworth Castle itself stands near the top of a 180m (600ft) conical hill on the eastern flank of the Pennines, two miles south of Barnsley. The Castle was built by Thomas Wentworth, Earl of Strafford of the second creation, after purchasing the estate from the Cutler family in 1708. Most of the Earl's early career was spent abroad representing Queen Anne as Special Ambassador in Berlin and the Hague, and he was familiar with, and influenced by, the highly formalised gardening styles being created in Europe at that time. After the death of Queen Anne in 1714, and the subsequent loss of Royal patronage, he devoted his enthusiasm and talent to the development of his large estate in South Yorkshire, although he had other large estates elsewhere.

By 1713 the Earl had begun work laying out the baroque garden in the manner of Versailles, as recommended to him by Loudon and Wise; a layout of geometric planned paths and avenues with long vistas. A second stage of the garden development was the building of a large gothic castle folly, Stainborough Castle, on the summit of the hill overlooking the grounds of Wentworth Castle. The towers of the castle folly dominated the landscape in every direction. Built from 1726–30, this was one of the first mock castles incorporated into an 18th century garden landscape. Two years later the Corinthian Temple was built overlooking the great south lawn. When the first Earl died in 1739 the estates and titles passed to his son William. The second Earl's approach to the garden was a more natural style, contrasting strongly with the severe formality of his father's creation.

Very few additions were made thereafter to the formal gardens until the mid 19th century when exotic trees and hardy hybrid rhododendrons were planted by Thomas Vernon-Wentworth (the title had by then become extinct).

A fine Paxton-style cast iron conservatory was added around 1840, built by Compton and Fowkes of Cheltenham, now listed Grade II and in dire need of extensive repair. In spite of its delapidation it houses a fine collection of mature *Camellia japonica*, planted in the late 19th century, also some *C. reticulata* hybrids planted in the last five years. Tender species and hybrid rhododendrons are also grown in pots and tubs, such as *R.* 'Fragrantissimum', *R. burmanicum*, *R. horlickianum*, *R. dalhousiae*, *R. lindleyi*, *R. rhabdotum* and others.

The last private owner, Capt. Bruce Vernon-Wentworth, was an avid collector of hardy hybrid rhododendrons and from 1902 to 1939 he planted novelties as they became available commercially, but he never saw fit to introduce species *Rhododendron, Magnolia, Camellia, Acer, Hamamelis* or *Pieris*. In 1919 the Captain planted a magnificent lime tree avenue which lines the side of the historical Lady Lucy's Walk and is now in its prime.

Throughout the Second World War Wentworth Castle was requisitioned and occupied by the army, resulting in a considerable amount of neglect and damage.

In 1948 the main house, gardens and parkland were sold to Barnsley Corporation for use as a teacher training college for women. This college was closed in 1978 and the site leased to the newly established Northern College for Adult Education. Faced with the responsibility for the upkeep of the grounds and gardens, the Northern College launched a major restoration programme, with myself in charge, financed as a Community Work Project by central government funds channelled through the MSC.

After decades of neglect stretching back to the First World War, indigenous trees such as holly, ash and sycamore had almost closed the canopy above the original collections of hardy hybrid rhododendrons. *R. ponticum* rootstocks of grafted hybrids had suckered and enveloped the lawns, paths and avenues with their invasive vigour, and overwhelmed

the less sturdy cultivars. With the help of 25 placements employed on the MSC scheme, we thoroughly cleared the 16 ha (40 acres) of all dead, diseased and unwanted plant material and carefully restored the lawns, paths and rides etc. exactly as depicted on our copy of the 1713 landscape plans. Three years later, having completed the clearances, I began to cultivate and replant the re-possessed areas. While retaining the best of the original trees, and the healthiest of the aged rhododendrons, a collection of species and modern hybrid rhododendrons was begun. Also for the first time *Magnolia, Camellia, Acer, Sorbus, Enkianthus, Eucalyptus, Betula, Kalmia, Eucryphia, Meconopsis* and Asiatic primulas were introduced to the gardens.

Sixteen years on we now have a very comprehensive collection of *Rhododendron* covering 16 ha (40 acres), from the very earliest hardy hybrids to the most recent introductions, along with our introduced species representing 34 sections (Cullen and Chamberlain revision 1980) and including 500 species and subspecies. Many of the species are named clones, award winners or have collector's seed numbers. For this enterprise we were awarded National Collection status from the National Council for the Conservation of Plants and Gardens (NCCPG). The collection is continually being added to as 'missing' species rhododendrons become available.

It is difficult to choose favourites from the many hundreds of rhododendrons grown here. The challenge always was, what could be satisfactorily grown on an exposed 180m (600ft) high Pennine hill with an Arctic winter climate, a very low summer rainfall and a miniscule budget.

The exotic, large-leaved species, the Falconera section, was experimented with first. Sites with well sheltered microclimates, open to a southerly aspect, were identified. These were cultivated by digging holes a cubic yard into the stratas of shale and stone, which lay inches below the soil surface. A planting compost of 50 per cent acid top soil and 50 per cent leafmould ensured a water-retentive medium in which the plants luxuriated. Our planting holes would act as a sump in wetter areas drowning the roots, but here they retain moisture throughout the drier seasons. A mulch of leafmould minimises evaporation, keeping the root system cool and making available a slow release of nutrients. Having mountains of leafmould available, decaying over a three-year period, is the life blood of our growing culture, common to all our plantings and has been vital for the survival of the living collection during the drought years.

Over a period of time all the species in the Falconera section were purchased as small plants and grown on in pots for several years in a frost-free environment until robust enough to be introduced into the open garden. Many years later, after a visit by the Collections Officer of the NCCPG, we were awarded the National Collection status for the Falconera section – a very satisfactory and surprising outcome to the original experiment. In tandem to the species, 15 clones of Loderi grex were successfully grown in the same manner as the Falconera. 'Venus', 'Gamechick', 'Julie', 'King George' and 'Pink Diamond' do extremely well, oblivious of our Arctic climate. They are very floriferous as well as scented, and obviously hardier than generally supposed. The Grandia section, however, has proved decidedly tender with only *R. macabeanum* and *R. praestans* proving robust, while several forms of *R. sinogrande* make only slow progress. A more recent introduction, *R. kesangiae* seems, after a few mild winters, so far to be quite hardy.

The Taliensia section is well represented with forms of *R. bureavii* and *R. elegantulum* especially good with fabulous rusty red indumentum. All forms of *R. yakushimanum* are splendid with 'Koichiro Wada' having the edge and worthy of its 1947 FCC Award. Another exceptional specimen of great beauty is *R. pachysanthum, RV2001*, now 3m (10ft) wide and 2.2m (7ft) high and of perfect symmetry, whose pollen is in some demand by hybridisers. *R. ramsdenianum* has grown to 5m (15ft) in as many years and in spite of its H3 hardiness rating, surprises visitors with its blood red blooms lasting from March to the end of April, often covered in snow. *R. mallotum* F17853 is another early to flower with the most gorgeous blooms of fleshy crimson and doubly welcome as it herals in the new spring. The first yellow species to brighten up the dark winter days is *R. lutescens* 'Bagshot Sands' of which quite a number have been propagated from cuttings, grown on, and eventually planted in front of dark backgrounds such as the black-green of yews. *R. sutchuenense, R. strigillosum, R. praevernum, R. oreodoxa* and *R. barbatum* are others that bring cheerful colour to the gardens in late winter.

Of the dwarf species, 60 are planted in a raised bed behind the conservatory; my favourites there being, *R. cephalanthum* Crebreflorum Group, *R. pumilum, R. sargentianum* 'Whitebait' and *R. campylogynum* 'Bodnant Red'. *R. ludlowii* too has a very beautiful flower and thrives in semi-shade in the deep humus-rich soil despite its reputation of being difficult. The rhododendron season is concluded early in August by the lovely scented white blossoms of *R. auriculatum* and the hybrids 'Iceberg' and 'Polar Bear'.

The first magnolia to be introduced, and also my favourite, was *M. sinensis* and is now growing quite strongly between specimens of *R. macabeanum* and *R. falconeri*. The flower of *M. sinensis* is a sheer delight with its pendant saucers of purest white, stunning bosses of crimson stamens and its powerful fragrance. This magnolia species is probably the most publicly admired and acclaimed flower in the whole living collection. The purchase of the other three species in the section Oyama, *M. sieboldii*, *M. wilsonii* and *M. globosa* soon followed and enthralled visitors with their exquisite beauty and scent.

When a long south-facing bank immediately below the folly castle became available, due to the onslaught of fierce gales felling shallow-rooted trees growing on shale and slabs of sandstone, we laboriously prepared our usual holes for new planting. In these holes 62 hybrid and species magnolia were planted along with a dozen or so camellias and *Halesia carolina*. Of the magnolias that have already flowered the intense deep yellow of 'Yellow Bird' is the most stunning flower, but many others are exceptionally beautiful in their own right. The de Vos and Kosar hybrids produce clouds of colour every spring. The eight 'little girls' do extremely well, more vigorous and floriferous than either of their parents, *M. liliiflora* 'Nigra' and *M. stellata* 'Rosea'. They also root easily from soft wood cuttings and are therefore widely planted around the gardens as well as on the Magnolia Bank. The earliest to flower is 'Ann', closely followed by 'Betty' and 'Susan', all in the month of April. 'Judy', 'Randy' and 'Ricki' bloom here two or three weeks later, with 'Jane' and 'Pinkie' ending the series flowering season in late May. Of the taller specimens, 'Crimson Stipple', 'Joe McDaniel' and 'Heaven Scent' all make an attractive display, well supported by the *M. × soulangeana* cultivars, 'Brozzoni', 'Lennei', 'Burgundy', 'Rustica Rubra', 'San Jose', 'Alba

Superba' and 'Alexandrina', all earning their keep with an explosion of colour. The *M. campbellii*, *M. sprengeri* var. *diva*, *M. dawsoniana*, and *M. kobus* are too young as yet to make flower. When viewed from above or below, the bank will be an unforgettable sight. Interplanting with camellias completes the colour scheme.

One of the most special secret places within the gardens is a large sunny glade, open to the south but heavily sheltered on the other sides by mature oak and yew blocking out the Arctic and Siberian weather that winter throws at them. The whole area is surrounded and kept secret by a dense wall of old hardy hybrid rhododendrons. Planted within it you find the magnolias 'Star Wars', 'Manchu Fan', *M. liliiflora* 'Nigra', 'Iolanthe' and *M. brooklynensis* 'Woodsman', 'Betty', 'Yellow Fever' and the queen of the show, *M. campbellii* subsp. *mollicomata* 'Lanarth'. Many of these are charmed into flower by the songs of the spring migrants; blackcap, willow warbler, pied flycatcher singing in their branches, a paradise of the senses – sight, sound and scent. Nearby *M. salicifolia* is a small twiggy tree festooned in white butterflies fluttering in the leafless branches. Elsewhere and adjacent to paths, three magnolias are putting all their energies into vegetative growth and making impressive trees – *M. officinalis* var. *biloba*, *M. sargentiana* var. *robusta* and 'Mark Jury'. All in all, 64 different hybrids and 44 species for which the NCCPG awarded National Collection status for species *Magnolia*.

In my early youth I believed those exotic beauties, the camellias, would not flourish in the North. This opinion was born out of the sight of those dead young specimens frequently seen blackened after the end of the winter, while visiting other large gardens and also the fact that none existed outdoors at

Wentworth Castle. I began their introduction by experimenting with the *C. × williamsii* cultivars, growing them on for two or three years in 30cm (12in) pots overwintered under glass. When the hardwood had ripened they were planted out into the usual holes among favourable sites in late spring. For a few winters each specimen would be surrounded by a protective wigwam of yew branches and bracken and mulched with leafmould to counter penetration by frost and ice. This cultivation technique proved to be 100 per cent successful. After one particularly hard winter, I was relieved that all the williamsii cultivars survived and, with renewed confidence, I brought in some japonica hybrids, all of which performed equally well. Those that come to mind as doing particularly well in the gardens are 'Lady Clare', 'Adolphe Audusson', 'Blaze of Glory', 'Contessa Lavinia Maggi', 'Elegans', 'Mrs D. W. Davies', and surprisingly, flowering in deep shelter, 'Mathotiana Alba'. Of the tougher williamsii my own favourites would include 'Anticipation', 'Bowbells', 'Brigadoon', 'Debbie', 'Donation', 'Elsie Jury', 'Joan Trehane', 'St Ewe' and 'Water Lily'.

Of the *C. reticulata* hybrids I would favour the crosses, 'Leonard Messel', 'Inspiration' and 'Dream Girl' and also the two 'bankers', *C. cuspidata × C. japonica*, 'Cornish Snow' and 'Cornish Spring'. If I had to choose but one camellia for this cold climate it would have to be the very outstanding 'Debbie'. But then, I would never want to be without that elegant beauty, 'Francis Hanger', either outdoors or under glass, an exquisite perfection of the purest white petals surrounding a boss of golden stamens whose simplicity I find enthralling.

An enchanting experience in spring is a leisurely stroll down the Camellia Walk to view the 52 cultivars blooming there under a light and high canopy of oak, pine and beech, interplanted with magnolias, *Eucryphia* 'Nymansay', azaleas, pieris, acers, eucalyptus, sorbus, ferns and smaller rhododendrons. The whole area becomes a kaleidoscope of colour, richly scented by nearby *Rhododendron* Loderi cultivars and enriched by the rapturous chorus of birdsong. Whether early morning or evening this is a place of the utmost serenity and tranquillity and a paradise found; a must for poets and painters.

Camellias feature again as an informal hedge around two sides of the large azalea gardens, with its extensive rockery creating an exciting harmony of contrasts, with the blues of the meconopsis, alpine campanula, corydalis, etc. against the pastel shades of numerous azaleas and the stronger hues of the camellias. Visitors are often very enthusiastic over two camellia cultivars – 'Jury's Yellow' and 'Brushfield's Yellow' and that white beauty with its pale blush cheeks, standing in the shadow, 'Hope'. Another attractive white, 'Bridal Gown', draws attention to the hedge looking lovely between 'Donation' and 'Blaze of Glory'.

To walk round this garden is an experience never to be forgotten as there is something for all tastes – the sheer beauty of the place and its situation, the sense of peace and tranquillity and of nature tamed and untamed in all its glory.

It has been a privilege to work in such surroundings. Few people are able to leave a monument to their life's work.

Derek Rogers MBE is a member of the Group, and, from 1978 until his recent retirement, he was in charge of the restoration of the gardens of Wentworth Castle. He remains an adviser to the Wentworth Castle Garden Trust

International Camellia Society Congress

Joey Warren

Japan is half a world away. My efforts to learn Japanese gave me only a few words of greetings and thanks but I did absorb some familiarity with Japanese voices, looks, customs, food, music. Many Japanese people wear western clothes (dark business suits) so there was no 'culture shock', just a huge appreciation of the kindness and courtesy that Japanese people show to foreigners as well as to each other. We stayed in large, western-style hotels in utmost comfort. The food was strange and fun, frequent and plentiful, and the water safe to drink. The coaches were smooth and comfortable and we were not crowded. Everywhere we were helped, advised, guided by cheerful staff and volunteers – lots and lots of them.

The organisational aspects of looking after over 600 people from 14 countries across the world attending the five-day Congress at Miyazaki, southern Kyushu, Japan, had been very well researched and planned. The event was managed by Miyazaki City Council jointly with the Japanese Camellia Society and the local branches. The reception desk at Miyazaki Kanko Hotel swarmed with staff (in yellow jackets) and interpreters (in red jackets) who accompanied the delegates on all visits and tours.

The Congress's welcome ceremony began with the President of the Japan Camellia Society, Mrs Tohko Adachi, creating an ikebana flower arrangement of camellias between a large bamboo frame (see Fig. 15). She glided across the stage in kimono and sash (*obi*), while a group of musicians played haunting Japanese music. There were speeches of welcome, and good wishes, supper, and then a performance of loud, vibrant drumming on one big barrel-like wooden drum high up on a stand, the rhythm slow at first then increasing in speed.

The camellia, a native of Japan and revered by the Japanese, is used medicinally and herbally for tea, soap and other toiletries, also as cooking oil, decoration, paintings and embroideries. The long curved rail in the atrium of the Miyazaki Kanko Hotel held a row of vases of individual named camellia hybrid flowers. And the hotel was decorated with camellias. The famous scroll 'Picture of One Hundred Camellias' in the Miyazaki Municipal Museum was on view with a fine collection of oil paintings of camellias.

There is a strong camellia society in Japan and 525 Japanese people attended the Congress together with 145 from other countries. We were welcomed by ladies of the Nobeoke Branch when we visited Shiro-yama Castle to see the camellias, which had been neglected over many years but were now re-instated through the work of a voluntary group. These very old, large camellia trees with single red or pale pink flowers were growing on high banks. And we were welcomed by the Hagi Branch at Torogasaki Camellia Grove, a 10-ha (245-acre) forest by the sea of 2,500 wild *Camellia japonica* trees, revered when planted, but then cut down regularly until, in 1965, a Japanese pharmacist researching the *Camellia* persuaded the Mayor of Hagi to let them grow. They are now accessible as a beautiful camellia forest. We were guided through paths among their bare trunks, sparse, single red or pink flowers overhead, to a high point overlooking the canopy.

Another forest we visited was the vast Tsubakiyama Forest Park on a steep hillside. There was a tree-planting ceremony, musicians played in a marquee, and there was a tea ceremony. I loved wandering in the warm rain in this forest among the huge planting of 40,000 camellias, mostly hybrids, including 70 species; the aim is to increase the planting to 100,000. It poured with rain and although we all had waterproof gear, we were given large plastic macs – such hospitality!

The planting of hybrid camellias at the Nagashima Art Gallery and Museum, on a high point overlooking Kagoshima City, is on an open site without much shade. The plants had grown well further downhill and become overcrowded, and been moved two years ago to this new bed, but they did not seem happy in their new position.

The Congress consisted of days out visiting camellia plantings, and one day of lectures in the Miyazaka Kanko Hotel. Papers had been printed beforehand, and were read, mostly by their authors, expanded and supported by slides. Translators into English, Japanese, French and German sat in booths at the back of the hall and earphones were easy to use. The Chairman was Vice-President Mr Shunpei Uemoto and everything was very well organised. The papers will appear in the next International Camellia Society (ICS) Yearbook; subjects were as follows

Habitats of Wild Camellia and Old Trees in Japan, by Shuho Kirino (Japan)

A Short History of Camellia Breeding in New Zealand, by Rod L Bieleski (New Zealand)

Camellias in Germany – Past and Present, by Waldemar Max Hansen (Germany)

White and Red Camellia at Nara's Todaiji Temple, by Kaoru Hagiya (Japan)

Research on Camellia Flower Blight in New Zealand, by Peter Long (New Zealand)

Simple Incision Grafting for Camellia, by Katsusuke Oota (Japan)

Camellias at Longwood Gardens, by William Thomas (USA)

The Comprehensive Presentation of Camellia japonica *in Korea*, by Sang Rea Lee (Korea)

The Origin and Development of the Williamsii Hybrids, by Jennifer Trehane (UK)

The apple camellia (*Camellia japonica macrocarpa*) only grows on the island of Yakushima, and its fruit has a very large thick pericarp. We spent one night on Yakushima, a 4-hour ferry ride south from Miyazaki. On arrival, we were driven up a newly constructed road to see very old apple camellia trees, with sparse, dark red single flowers, but no fruits. We passed a family of monkeys and appreciated the engineering work which stabilises the precipitous, forested roadsides, and prevents landslides.

Yakushima is a steep mountain with four peaks, the highest being Mt Miyanoura, 1,935m (6,350ft), which is cut by ravines, 35.5km (22 miles) across north to south and 45km (28 miles) across east to west, with a very narrow, flat coastal strip. It receives a huge amount of rain, and supports a great number of plant species as it is sub-tropical at sea level, but the temperature drops with height and this creates a very wide range of temperatures and wet/drier conditions to suit a very large range of plants. Ferns and mosses are everywhere. The island lies about 64km (40 miles) south of the southernmost tip of Kyushu, Japan's most southerly major island. Bush camellias (*C. japonica*) grow in the narrow coastal flat strip with the broad-leaved evergreens, while the apple camellia grows at between 500–1,300m (1,600–4,300ft) height with the deciduous trees and conifers. The botanic garden in the grounds of our hotel was a wonderland of plants twixt mountain and sea – strelitzias, musa, orchids, tree ferns, callistemons, hibiscus – a wide range familiar as outdoor and greenhouse plants but all growing side by side.

Yakushima is also the only home of *Rhododendron yakushimanum* (see Fig. 16), which grows at the top of the island above the tree line, but we could not go so high. Indeed the road ended at the apple camellias, continuing only as a forest track. We did, however, see a film on a huge cinema screen in the Museum of the whole of the island. Taken from a helicopter, it showed the Sen'piro Waterfalls and ravine then swooped over the four peaks, to where, on the top, above the tree line, were the perfect, dome-shaped bushes of *R. yakushimanum.*

We were also taken to see very big, very old *Cryptomeria japonica* trees, the Japanese cedars. This tree is used for everything: timber construction work, furniture, tools, carvings, all small items of wood. It even has medicinal properties and is planted widely throughout Japan; in fact we saw forests of it everywhere we went. Some were beside the apple camellias, a quarter of the way up the mountain, some in Silago Gajumaru Forest park, with paths and swinging bridges over small ravines. Here, also, was Wilson's Stump

(believed to have been felled in 1914 for E H Wilson). Japanese Cedars 1,000 years old are called *yaku-sugi*; those even older are called *kigen-sugi*. At the *Cryptomeria japonica* Museum we were shown a slice from one which has 1,660 annual rings, and there were a photograph of one 3,000 years old, or even older (there was talk of 7,000 years old!).

On tour, on the Ebino Plateau high in the mountains west of Miyazaki, we saw scrubby bushes which could have been azaleas or maybe *R. kiusianum.* A plaque showing the magenta flowers that bloom there confirmed that they were azaleas.

At Agurikaracha Park, Edo, after the tree-planting ceremony we visited four private gardens in a leafy suburb of large, well-to-do houses, very different from the tiny houses which were seen everywhere else. Edo has been a camellia growing centre for 200 years. In the first garden we saw an original *Camellia japonica* 'Donckelaari' (*C. japonica* 'Masayoshi'), named after M Donckelaar, one time Director of the Royal Gardens at Ghent. It has large semi-double, red marbled white flowers. We also met a delightful old lady of 93 who had been gardening all her life. The second garden, behind a temple, had some 200-year-old *Camellia japonica* (known as *yabu tsubaki*) with single red flowers on very tall trees, also *higo tsubaki* which was 120 years old. We walked to and around the other two private gardens, full of camellias, and felt very privileged to have enjoyed their peaceful atmosphere.

A 'highlight' of the Conference programme was to visit a private home, as a way of promoting friendly relationships. My husband John and I were hosted by Mr Hidara, who owns a small printing business. Mrs Hidara shares the work, as does their 16-year-old son when not at college. The reception room is above the works and we went there first for introductions and green tea. Then we had a tour of the printing works and met all eight employees. We then visited their small house a few yards down the street. After we shed shoes for the waiting slippers, we sat at a low table on floor cushions, legs straight out in front, which was difficult. We had done this once before at a barbecue-style lunch which we hated. Everything was very clean, neat and small – most Japanese people are small and slender. A shrine of Buddha in the corner dwarfed the room. Everything was made of wood and the floor was covered with close-woven reed matting. The language was difficult, as Mr Hidara had a few words of English, his son more, Mrs Hidara none. There was more green tea, and a very pleasant exchange of gifts, lots of goodwill and smiles and bowing. Mr Hidara's sister arrived, she is a Vice-President of the Aoshima Island Hotel and spoke some English. We moved into the small, modern kitchen onto bench-seating round a higher kitchen table, and sister began to cook in a deep electric fryer, with olive oil, garlic, onion, tomatoes, green vegetables, lettuce and finally thin strips of beef. The table already groaned with food – raw fish, cooked fish, vegetables, salads, pickles, marinated foods, fruit. It was all delicious and we ate heartily, but there was a lot left untouched. Sister entertained us by making tiny Origami paper animals. I tried out some Japanese language, and that amused them, and we spent the rest of the evening writing words on paper – a little lesson – and were all entertained. It was a happy evening.

We explored Miyazaki, walking along the riverbank garden to Tachibana Street, the main street. *Phoenix canariensis* is the symbol of Miyazaki and the streets and avenues are lined with them, or with palms (*Livistona* species) . At least eight gardeners were work-ing close together in a huddle, planting out bedding plants into new beds. Everywhere we went we saw carefully laid out beds of annual bedding plants – Iceland poppies, begonias, geraniums, balotta, tagetes, violas, often in garish colours. Their tools were made of bamboo. At the Peace Museum Park in Hiroshima again we saw 8–10 gardeners, squatting in a huddle on a small area of grass, teasing out moss thatch by hand with bamboo forks, and the area of grass was immense. The gardeners all wore clogs, and the lady gardeners all wore bonnets tied on with scarves.

After visiting the Shrine of the First Emperor, in Miyazaki, we walked through evergreen woodland to a Greenery Fair, held for a month, each March and September. All round the edges of a large open space, nurseryman from Kyushu had come to sell their plants, making small demonstration gardens. We loved seeing all the plants that grow there, many were tender, greenhouse plants to us – *Hibiscus, Bougainvillea, Cycas, Dicksonia* but many were familiar garden plants – *Spiraea*, roses, *Fuchsia, Photinia, Daphne*, tree peonies. Most remarkable was the pruning, the shaping of plants, which came in all sizes, small alpines to large, and large shaped, evergreen trees, roots wrapped in hessian or bamboo, costing £1,000 and more.

The Bullet Train (Shinkansen) whisked us from Hiroshima to Kyoto, through flat land, and tunnel after tunnel – wherever there was a hill, a tunnel went through it. The countryside is either very flat, or steep volcanic mountain side . The mountains are forested, mainly with *Cryptomeria japonica* and bamboo; very few people live in the mountains. The flat land is lived on, and intensively cultivated. The houses are very small, so are the gardens. We saw acres and acres of polytunnels with cucumber, tomatoes, capsicum, mangoes, tobacco and Japanese 'Unshu' oranges. They grow lots of vegetables and salad crops and fruit. We saw tea plantations, like long, thick hedges with narrow gaps between them, harvested mechanically; electric fans above the *Camellia sinensis* on 3m (10ft) poles keep air moving and prevent frost damage. Rice is grown in small, wet fields, surrounded by low banks, and is also sown and harvested mechanically – though they are cutting back on their rice production and buying from abroad. They like to eat sticky rice. We were told that fishing is mainly for tuna, mackerel and lobster – prawns, too, perhaps.

We had a wonderful two and a half weeks and the tourist visits in Kyoto included the Imperial Palace, with its serene evergreen gardens, and arched bridge reflected in the still pond; the Nijo-jo Castle, with groves of cherry trees just beginning to blossom; the Golden Pavilion; Kiyomizu-Dera Temple; museums, art galleries, gift shops, and much much more. And everywhere the welcome was total and sustained.

Joey Warren is the Honorary Secretary of the Group and a member of the Executive Committee. She lives in Devon

PHOTOGRAPHIC COMPETITION

There was an excellent response to the request for more entries, so that the Judges were faced with a wide variety of prints and slides, and also of subject matter. It proved to be a close contest and far from easy to come to a decision. Congratulations are due to all who decided to enter. In the end the winner of the £25 cheque was Mr J D Bottle with his well composed picture of *R. niveum* 'Crown Equerry' (see Fig. 22). Second was a French member of the Group M J-P Chatelard with *Magnolia* 'Gretl Eisenhut', taken in P van Veen's Swiss garden (see Fig. 23). Third equal was Mr Hargreaves with *R. taggianum* 'Harry Tagg' taken at Arduaine (see Fig. 24) and Mr J D Bottle with *R. bureavii* (see Fig. 25). All four photographs, as is customary, have been printed in this issue of the Year Book.

Two further entries have been printed for their general interest – M Chatelard's picture of *Magnolia campbellii* subsp. *mollicomata* 'Werrington' (see back cover), less familiar than *M.* 'Lanarth', but raised from the same Forrest seed no. 25655; and Mrs Jean Arblaster's picture of a cross made by her late husband in 1984 between *R.* 'New Comet' (syn 'Emerald Isle') and *R. caloxanthum* (see Fig. 32).

The support for the competition from a wide range of the membership was most heartening, and it is hoped that those good or especially interesting slides or prints taken in 1999 or 2000 will not be forgotten or mislaid, but entered next year for the 2001 issue competition.

THE REBIRTH OF MAGNOLIA SARGENTIANA VAR. ROBUSTA AT HIGH BEECHES GARDENS

ANNE BOSCAWEN

This great magnolia, one of the most beautiful of all flowering trees, fell in the great storm of October 1987. High Beeches was full in the eye of the storm, and this was perhaps the most grievous loss. We were lucky to lose only one rhododendron, *R. diaprepes* F11958. We tried to pull it up, but it twisted and fell again.

Magnolia sargentiana var. *robusta* was 11m (36ft) high, by Tree Register measurement in 1987, bushy and very heavily branched. We discussed trying to pull it upright, but there was nothing substantial enough to which we could attach a winch, and we decided that we were unlikely to succeed. There is always a danger of twisting and breaking the remaining roots.

With so much else to attend to, we let it lie until the spring of 1988, when it burst into bloom on every twig! This was an amazing sight, but our raptures were tempered by the knowledge that it might be its death throw. Experts who saw it then told us that we had one of the very few remaining 'Chenault' trees, with flowers of rare and sumptuous beauty.

In 1988 we covered the exposed root with ten loads of topsoil, and in subsequent years, the top and branches died back, but hundreds of epicormic shoots sprouted from the main trunk. It does not seem to layer itself,

although some branches are in contact with the ground.

This year it flowered again, if possible more spectacularly than ever, on every shoot (see Figs. 18 and 19). It lasted in beauty several weeks, the flowers as lovely as before. It made a stunning sight, even for those accustomed to the beauty of the genus as a whole.

The tree is listed in our records as *M. sargentiana* var. *robusta*. It first flowered in 1955, 27 years after it was first planted. William Stockton, son of the gardener, can remember this as a tremendously notable event. Many photographs were taken then, but we know of none surviving.

Colonel Loder, who planted it in 1928, constantly refers in the records to his tree being 'worked', i.e. grafted, but he does not give the source. He was understandably impatient for it to flower, and notes the date of first flowering, and the height at 6m (20ft) in 1942. It was 11m (36ft) high in 1987. The leaves are uniformly and distinctly notched at the apex. They also, alone among our many magnolias, 'skeletonise' themselves. The charming 'fairy wings' can be picked up beneath the tree at any time.

Ernest Wilson found *M. sargentiana* var. *robusta* in 1910, on the Wa-shan in Szechwan, at 2,300m (7,600ft), while collecting seed for the Arnold Arboretum. Dr

Sargent, then the Director, germinated the seed, but decided that the plants would not be hardy on the East Coast of America, and sent them to Chenaults Nursery, of Orleans, France. From there, a few grafted plants were distributed, and fewer still, perhaps three or four, survive today. One has been identified at Lanarth, Cornwall.

Later introductions are not nearly so good. The original wild source has never been rediscovered, and this form is probably extinct in the wild.

An old *Prunus sargentii*, which was planted in 1914, only 2.5m (8ft) away, died of honey fungus five years ago. The fungus has not, apparently, yet infected the magnolia, which is now being propagated. Efforts at grafting, made by several nurseries in 1988, have so far failed.

References

GARDINER, J M, (1989). *Magnolias*. Cassell, London.

BEAN, W J, (1973). *Trees and Shrubs Hardy in the British Isles*. 8th Ed Vol II. John Murray, London.

HUNT, D, (1998). *Magnolias and their allies*, IDS/TMS conference proceedings. Illustration p.259, J Gardiner. The International Dendrology Society.

Anne Boscawen and her husband Edward, both members of the Group, have restored and extended the garden at The High Beeches, now High Beeches Conservation Trust, at Handcross in W Sussex

THE HARDY HYBRID
RHODODENDRON COLLECTION

MIRANDA GUNN AND JOHN BOND

Ramster and the Hardy Hybrid Collection

The garden at Ramster is situated on the edge of the Weald, on the borders of Surrey and West Sussex and was first laid out between 1890 and 1920 by Sir Harry Waechter. He converted the Elizabethan farmhouse to the present house, and created the gardens and lakes out of an oak wood, which extend over some 8 ha (20 acres). He was fortunate to have, on adjoining land, the then famous nursery Gauntletts of Chiddingfold whom he employed to design and plant his woodland garden. Many of the oaks have now matured into fine specimens, and provide us with excellent overhead canopy under which the garden flourishes. The soil is acid to neutral, and consists of Wealden clay, with pockets of sand. The rainfall averages 80cm (32.5in) a year.

My grandparents bought the property in 1922. My grandmother, daughter of the first Lord Aberconway, was a keen gardener, and, having been brought up at Bodnant, particularly passionate about rhododendrons. She was an early member of the Rhododendron Association. Her planting notes show that during the late 1920s and early 1930s hundreds of seedlings were sent down from Bodnant with Forrest, Kingdon Ward and Rock collectors' numbers, and also much seed. She lists, with notes on their performance, 76 species she had growing here, plus 43 'good hybrids, not counting others and azaleas'. She also made endless crosses of her own. But sadly the war brought much of this activity in the garden to an end, and as my grandmother and her three faithful gardeners got older, the garden was left gently ticking over, and became more and more overgrown.

When my husband Paul and I first started tentative forages into the garden in 1970 about 2 ha (5 acres) of the garden was covered with impenetrable bamboo forest, and another acre with Japanese knotweed. We found a few of the species that had survived, but the bulk of the rhododendrons were hybrids, including many huge bushes of hardy hybrids, which flowered indomitably year after year, giving a troublefree and reliable framework for the garden. As we battled our way round the garden, on a steep learning curve, we developed an affection for these splendid old plants and so we are now delighted if we can help towards their preservation.

On a rising slope at the end of the garden at Ramster was a woodland area, of some 2 ha (5 acres), containing some fine but neglected oak trees, some sweet chestnut, and a mass of self-sown ash, pubescent birch, chestnut and hazel, coppiced long ago, some holly, much fallen timber, and several enormous stumps. Paul and I had long been aware of the potential of this site, if we could ever get round to developing it, as it rises to the highest point in the garden, and would reveal new views of the garden and surrounding countryside. It also holds the reservoir, which stores the water for the garden pumped up from the lake by our Victorian ram pump. It was when the roof of the reservoir finally collapsed, after dangling dangerously for several years, that we took the bit between our teeth and hacked through the impenetrable brambles and fallen trees to rebuild it. Once we had an access path, and a clear area on top of the hill, we could see that it was not an insuperable task to clear further, as the floor of the wood, completely shadowed by the close grown top storey, was fairly clear of undergrowth. Thus project Ant Wood was started, 'Ant' in memory of my uncle Antony Norman who had made such a success of developing my grandmother's other garden the Chateau de la Garoupe, at Antibes, where we spent so many happy gardening days.

We started carving out rides wide enough to give the tractor access, clearing scrub and small trees. Together with Stephen Blackman, our gardener, we drew up a plan of where the paths should go, where the view points would be, where grassy glades would be best, and outlining the planting areas. It was the biggest planning project we had ever undertaken, and we were a little daunted by the size of the undertaking, and the 'blank canvas' we had before us.

It was at this stage that during a Committee meeting of the RHS Rhododendron, Camellia and Magnolia Group the Chairman, John Bond, while discussing future plans for the group, suggested that we should try to find somewhere to create a collection of hardy hybrid rhododendrons. I pricked up my ears, and thought of my wood. This would give our project a worthwhile purpose, and surely hardy

hybrids would flourish there. What a challenge, if the wood was considered suitable, to make a collection of these splendid plants. John came to visit the wood, and thought it would be suitable for his project. So we devised a plan whereby the Group would purchase the plants which we, together with a small band of volunteers, would look after. Members of the Group would then have free access to Ramster Gardens, when they were open to the public. The Committee agreed to the proposal, and generously voted £2,000 to make the first purchase of plants.

We set to work on the first 1 ha (2.5 acres) of the wood with renewed purpose. Weeks of hard work followed, over 60 trees were felled, logged, and chipped. Scrub was cleared and burnt, leggy old rhododendrons dug up, the local tree surgeon tidied up all the good trees and removed dangerous branches. Paths were bulldozed through and sandstone laboriously laid down and rolled in. The whole area was rabbit fenced, and gates installed. Finally the grass paths and glades were seeded and all the planting areas broken up with a digger, as there is virtually no topsoil in the wood, and the ground is much too hard to dig by hand. Apart from occasional help from Paul and me, all this was done by our splendid 'in-house' team of two.

Finally in December 1998, Stephen and I drove the trailer over to collect nearly 200 plants of 71 different hardy hybrid rhododendrons from Knaphill Nurseries, where Martin Slocock has given the Group much help and encouragement with the project.

Then on a fine day in February, following much heavy rain, a group of volunteers from the Wessex Branch gathered to start the exciting task of planting (see Fig. 20). Even though it had been broken up the soil was still very heavy, and in some places completely waterlogged. We used a mixture of well-rotted horse manure, leafmould and wood chippings as a mulch, and at the end of a long morning, 200 strong young plants adorned the wood.

A considerable number flowered this May, and now six months on, having been deadheaded, weeded, rotavated, mulched, watered and generally fussed and worried over, nearly all the plants are thriving. We are looking forward to providing them with some companion plants and some labels this year, before we tackle another section of the wood. Ant Wood, and the collection of hardy hybrid rhododendrons will be opening to the public on 4 June, 2000, and we do hope many members of the Group will come and visit it.

Miranda Gunn

The Hardy Hybrid Project

When I became Chairman of the Group almost three years ago there were many requests that we should do more for the *Rhododendron*. Obviously these were creditable requests; after all that is the basic reason for our existence. There were suggestions, although not very helpful ones, such as send someone to China to collect seed – we have been back into the area for 20 plus years and sadly there is not a lot to show for the thousands of packets collected during that period. Produce more books we were told, but following the publication of the royal Horticultural Society's *Rhododendron Handbook*, Peter Cox's outstanding last book and our Group's *Rhododendron Story*, there is nothing required at the present time. There were a few other suggestions, which were even less relevant.

Many small rhododendron societies throughout the world have or have attempted to develop a rhododendron garden and most of these societies find that the running of these particularly hard work, both from the financial situation and the problem of the volunteer workers. There was no question of us starting a garden, for our finances, although healthy, are far too small. The idea of collections placed in appropriate existing gardens was put before the executive committee and this idea found favour.

Many of us have long been aware of the fact that the hardy hybrid rhododendron was fast disappearing in the trade and this group of plants became our first choice. A home for this collection was found at Ramster (see note above) and in 1998 some 70 hybrids have been planted in ones, twos, threes and fours.

I am often asked what are the guide lines of this particular venture, for, as I am informed frequently there are a host of hardy hybrid rhododendrons.

Firstly let us consider the breeding. Here we are talking of those hybrids derived from *R. arboreum, R. ponticum, R. catawbiense, R. maximum, R. campanulatum*, and, most important of all, *R. griffithianum*. In the main, the breeding work was carried out between 1830 and 1900 when the species listed above became available.

The hybridists of the day also provide us with another important guideline and here the list includes Waterers of Bagshot and Waterers of Knaphill, the various owners of Sunningdale Nurseries and Slococks of Woking. Important and very similar work was carried out at Boskoop in Holland and here the names of Endtz, Koster and Van Nes were very much to the fore.

My prediction at the outset of this venture was that we should perhaps be able to purchase 20–30 different hybrids. I failed to reckon with Martin Slocock's great effort at Knaphill Nurseries where he still grows a remarkable collection of this group of rhododendron's and from where we were able to purchase 70 different hybrids and there will be (we are told) more for us this year.

In spite of the great help we have been given we shall soon run out of plants in nurseries and we shall then organise a propagation programme which inevitably will slow us down considerably. A small committee/workforce has been formed, mainly from the Wessex Branch who are available to help with planting, labelling, deadheading, weeding and general help. These local members will also be responsible for tracing named hybrids and hopefully help with the propagation.

All Group members will be allowed free entry to Ramster during the garden's normal opening times and it is planned to open the collection area in late spring 2000.

John Bond

Miranda Gunn is a member of the Group and Chairman of the Wessex Branch.
John Bond is Chairman of the Group's Executive Committee and also a member of the Council of the RHS

Alan Hardy VMH

A man with a great sense of fun. A man with a great sense of duty. A man with a great love of the country and in particular his estate at Sandling in East Kent and a man with an ever greater love of horticulture. This sums up briefly Alan Hardy who sadly died earlier this year.

Alan inherited Sandling Park, which is comprised of a sizeable area of farm and woods, a large kitchen garden and an extremely well stocked woodland garden, from his father. When Alan took control of the garden it contained an exceptional collection of hardy hybrid rhododendrons together with an interesting range of companion trees and shrubs. He promptly extended the interest and seasonal colour by adding many rhododendron species and choicer hybrids together with more companion plants.

Above: Alan Hardy judging a rhododendron competition

Sadly, Sandling Park, being in a very exposed position, took the full brunt of the 1987 storm and virtually all of the valuable top canopy was lost, leaving a scene of seemingly total destruction. Many would have flinched from the rebuilding of a garden from such a scene. This was certainly not the case for Alan and Carolyn Hardy (and here I must make it clear that gardening at Sandling was always a very happy husband and wife team effort) who quickly mustered what forces they had at their disposal and began the massive clearing up operation. The

planting of shade trees was the first and urgent priority and the many British natives, North American red oaks in great variety, magnolias, maples and much else soon began to show their worth. There is a sad note to be made here, for, by the time of Alan's death, all of these had attained reasonable sizes and were 'working' and he was unable to enjoy his exciting new look garden.

Sandling was by no means the only horticultural interest of Alan's for he gave tremendous service to the Royal Horticultural Society, and obviously gained much pleasure from this involvement, over a very long period. It was in fact his interest in daffodils that first took him to Vincent Square and membership of the Daffodil Committee soon followed his arrival. This was followed by membership of Floral 'B'

Committee and of course the Rhododendron Committee. More recently he was a very much-valued founder member of the Woody Trials Committee. In recognition of his great service to horticulture and the Society Alan was awarded the Victoria Medal of Honour in 1993. Alan's great strength and great love was without doubt the *Rhododendron*; his knowledge was encyclopedic, particularly of the species.

Here should be mentioned his particular speciality, collection numbers, and it is entirely due to his efforts that we have such a thorough listing in the new RHS *Rhododendron Handbook*.

Lastly his great involvement with the Rhododendron Group must be mentioned. Alan was a member of the Executive Committee for many years and held various offices over that period; he also fought and worked with others extremely hard for the survival of the group through the difficulties of the early 1970s.

Perhaps those reading this obituary may find it appropriate to read the first paragraph again. Alan will be and is being greatly missed.

John Bond

THE MAGNOLIA SOCIETY

Offering members two color journals each year,
informative newsletters, a Seed Counter, Round Robins,
an annual convention, and knowledgeable members joined
in celebration of our favorite genus.

Membership includes all the above for $20, US; $25, Canada
and all other locations. Life memberships at $400.
All rates in U.S. dollars; VISA/MC accepted.

For membership or information regarding publications
or other services, please contact
Hazel Tarpley, Treasurer
5637 South Ryan Street
Seattle, Washington 98178-2296 USA

Sir Giles Loder Bt, VMH

To inherit a garden of the calibre of Leonardslee while still at school must have been daunting indeed. Sir Giles Loder, who died earlier this year aged 84, found himself in just that situation in 1920 when his grandfather died and he inherited the title and the Leonardslee estate, his father having been killed in the First World War. The picture outlined above is not quite accurate for Giles' mother 'held the fort' until he was of an age and in a position to take control.

I am sure that most of our members are familiar with Leonardslee but for those who have not had the pleasure of a visit, a brief description of the garden may be helpful. This I trust will help to set the scene which will illustrate Giles and his wife Marie's involvement in 'hands on' horticulture.

The garden lies in a deep valley, which contains a most attractive chain of Hammer Ponds, a relic from the time when iron and steel were produced in the area. The fairly sharply rising banks of the valley are liberally planted with a wide range of rhododendron hybrids, many of which were bred on the estate. Among these are the *Rhododendron* Loderi cultivars, bred by Giles' grandfather, Sir Edmund Loder in 1900, and which stand supreme. For this hybrid is arguably the finest rhododendron hybrid ever raised. Magnolias also play a very important role,

together with many other fine woodlanders in the overall scene.

During the 1970s and 1980s, Giles added a very large collection of hybrids of *Rhododendron yakushimanum* which provided the many visitors to the garden with a great amount of colour and most valuable study planting. It was, however, the great range of post war bred camellia cultivars that Giles and Marie gathered together from the USA, New Zealand, Australia and of course the UK, that was to become so important. These were grown both in the woodland and in two large glasshouses, and it was from this collection that many Gold Medal displays were shown at Royal Horticultural Society flowers shows at Vincent Square.

You will be aware from the above notes that Giles Loder was a very involved gardener. He was also for 50 or so years deeply involved in RHS work, serving on Council, the Rhododendron Committee, Floral 'B' Committee and very much more. For his great service to horticulture he was awarded the Victoria Medal of Honour, for his work with rhododendrons, the Loder Cup and was also made a Vice President of the RHS.

Finally mentions must be made of his great involvement with our Group where he gave unstinting support over many years and is very much missed.

John Bond

Rhododendron Group Tour, East and West Sussex, 6-10 May, 1999

Cynthia Postan

The annual tour has long been a feature of the Group's activities and almost every corner of the British Isles has been explored, often more than once. 1999 was no exception, offering the participants a chance to see some well-known gardens in East and West Sussex, as well as five notable private gardens. On 6 May 1999 12 members of the Group assembled at noon at the Winston Manor Hotel, Crowborough, to be joined the following day by another three members. A smaller number than usual, but all agreed that we thus had a unique opportunity to appreciate the discourse of the owners or curators, who accompanied us and generously told and showed us much that we might otherwise have missed.

Our first visit was to Sheffield Park which many of us had seen at the autumn weekend in the immediate aftermath of the great storm of October 1987. A great swathe of mature oaks had been carried away on the high ground but my memory is that the lake and valley with the precious *Nyssa sylvatica*, the tupelo, had to some extent been spared. Nigel Davis, now in charge of this domain, told us that Arthur Soames who planted the N American tree with its glorious autumn colour had given 180 plants to Westonbirt. He also told us this late-leafing tree was hardy up to the Canadian border.

Azaleas, especially the National Collection of Ghents now returning to general esteem, are one of the prides of this garden and were approaching their best, although a recent hard frost had damaged some of the Japanese evergreen varieties. We saw a bed of *Azalea rustica plena* (double flowered) newly planted in memory of Alan Hardy, so closely associated with our Group – a splendid memorial for such a colourful personality. In an effort to restore the Ghents to their own roots, Jim Inskip is propagating seedlings and cuttings, many of which come from James Russell's original Sunningdale collection which he moved to Ray Wood at Castle Howard. (See Nigel Davis's article, *Rhododendrons with Camellias and Magnolias*,1998, p.22). There were of course many other trees and rhododendrons for us to notice as we walked around the lake in glorious sunshine: *R.* 'Angelo' and 'Blue Peter' took my fancy as did a splendid specimen of the five-needled *Pinus montezumae* – always my favourite pine tree. We were grateful to Nigel for giving us so much of his time.

To round off the afternoon, we visited an intriguing private garden, Clinton Lodge, Fletching. No rhododendrons, alas, but what a tribute to the creative imagination of Mrs H Collum who kindly took us round. Not a large garden, but one divided into many separate compartments recreating garden history, all contained in clipped hedges, walls and even a camomile walk, while the surrounding country was framed by a newly planted pleached lime avenue. The diversity of plants was bewildering. Mrs Collum, whose creation it is, explained to us how the garden had developed from virtually nothing.

Friday morning took us to Leonardslee, well known to us all, but at the very peak of its glory. Robin Loder, one of the many Loders who have set their seal on British gardening, devoted most of his morning showing us the highlights. On the way he diverted us by many personal anecdotes. He told us of the low rainfall (73cm/28½in) and the dangers of frost, to avoid which air drainage was essential (the garden had recently to be closed because of frost damage, although the subsequent two weeks saw 25cm/10in of new growth); likewise, long ago, in 1907 a frost on the shortest night of the year had killed even the bracken). But his most intriguing stories were of the hybrids originating in the garden, notably the Loderi cultivars. He told us the seedlings grown on from the original seedpan had all collected awards, a remarkable record. Among these numerous cultivars we saw 'Pink Coral' with a huge trunk and 'Sir Edmund', pink, the original plant. Another Leonardslee hybrid, 'White Glory' ('Loderi' × *R. irroratum*) was in flower in late March this year on the day Robin's father, Sir Giles, died. We saw many 100-year-old trunks and some pre-1810 specimens, including a giant 190-year-old 'Cornish Red', which may have been there before the house was built. Among notable plants we saw *R. campylocarpum* × 'Idealist' (yellow), 'Hawk Crest', *R. spinuliferum*, *R. serpyllifolium*, really an azalea, with thyme-like leaves, *Embothrium* (cut down every few

years in this garden), and a 31.5m (105ft) *Metasequoia glyptostroboides.* He praised a bulb, *Liliohyacinth*, which flowers two weeks before the bluebell. He also, like so many other garden owners, spoke movingly of the great storm, although stressing that it enabled the garden, as he put it, 'to be brought into the 21st century'. A visit to the Rockery was a startling experience: those who know the Punchbowl at the Windsor Valley Gardens will realise the latter has stiff competition. Where else would you see azaleas including Wilson's Kurume 50 in such glorious clashing colours? After that a visit to Christopher Loder's excellent nursery ended our tour. Christopher's catalogue of species and hybrids, all grown to perfection outdoors, most without the help of polytunnels, is well worth writing for. Being there was a temptation not to be resisted. Thank you Robin and Christopher for much pleasure; you could not help the drizzling rain.

A quick sandwich and then into the coach for the short drive to High Beeches. Here we were greeted by Edward and Anne Boscawen, worthy successors to another branch of the Loder family. Anne's short introduction put the garden into its Loder context, but surely the tour that followed demonstrates how the Boscawens have made the most of their inheritance. This part of the Weald, with its natural tree cover, deep combes and frequent springs which lend themselves to man-made lakes, is a superb background for their enthusiasm. High Beeches is full of rhododendrons, many of them old and unusual, both hybrid and species, as the prizes on the RHS showbench testify, but surely the collection of rare tree specimens is what sets this woodland garden apart from others. I can only mention a few that we saw, all of intrinsic interest to a dendrologist. *Quercus myrsinifolia*, the bamboo-leaved oak, *Meliosma myriantha* from China, rare in the UK, *Quercus oxyodon* from the Himalayas, only here and at Caerhays in Cornwall, *Ilex latifolia*, the Himalayan holly with huge evergreen leaves, *Nothofagus fusca* from New Zealand: the list could be much, much longer. All these are beloved of the Boscawens. My account of this garden would, alas, not be complete without recounting the accident to our faithful 'tourist', Mac Speed, who was unlucky enough to slip on, of all unexpected plants, some bluebell leaves. Anne's head gardener, Chris Wardle, speedily summoned the ambulance and Mac spent several nights at the Haywards Heath Hospital. It is sad that Mac is having to spend some time in plaster. We missed him and his knowledgeable comments, and did our best to cheer up Helen who of course missed the remainder of the tour. Latest news of Mac is that he progresses well.

As if we had not seen enough to fill our notebooks, we then went on to Nymans, the old home of the Messel family, also famous for a garden created 100 years ago by Ludwig Messel. His son, Leonard, has both a camellia and a magnolia called after him. For 58 years James Comber, father of Harold, the collector of South American plants, was head gardener here. His present successor, David Masters, is Warden for the National Trust and we were most grateful for his articulate and informative narrative as he led us round the garden as it now is. Approached by a long conifer avenue, the pinetum was badly affected by the great storm, losing at least 350 trees. Trees we saw included *Keteleeria davidiana* found in central and west China by Père David, *Pinus montezumae* again (both conifers), *Crinodendron hookerianum* introduced from Chile by William Lobb, a superb Japanese wisteria seen throughout the garden

as well as twisting and turning on the ruins of the old house itself, *Prostanthera* species, *Hakea* species, both from Australasia, a sheltered area for large-leaved rhododendrons, such as *R. macabeanum* and *R. calophytum*, *Davidia involucrata* (showing us its white handkerchiefs) and many others. The garden layout is extensive and the croquet lawn and pergola with the Japanese wisteria is neighbour to the Heather Garden created in 1903, with its knoll and stone Japanese lanterns. It was too early for the wonderful borders and rose garden. Thank you David for making us so welcome.

Next day a long drive to West Sussex, a world away from the Weald, and visits to three smaller gardens, each quite distinctive in its own way. Mrs J Lakin's garden at Hammerwood near Midhurst is secluded and full of interesting plants – *Cornus alternifolia* and *C. controversa*, *Acer pseudoplatanus* 'Simon-Louis Frères' with pink-striped young leaves, *Aesculus pavia* 'Atrosanguinea', red Buckeye, a rarity, also *A. × mutabilis* 'Induta' and *Camellia japonica* 'Nuccio's Jewel'. Sweeping lawns led up to a bank of azaleas, Japanese and *R. luteum*. The house was draped in Banksia roses and ceanothus. After lunch to The Malt House at Chithurst, last visited in 1993, the home of Mr and Mrs Graham Ferguson (*Rhododendrons with Camellias and Magnolias*, 1994, p.63). Many of the plants there mentioned were seen in flower today, including *Cornus florida* 'Cherokee Chief', a striking brick red, and the Banksian rose. On the steep azalea bank several fine *R. yakushimanum* hybrids, such as 'Amanda Sue' and 'Percy Wiseman', clumps of *Lithodora* (syn. *Lithospermum*) and *R. spinuliferum*, the latter having suffered from the late frost. There were plants of *R. obtusum* f. *amoenum* var. *coccineum*, in particular, of considerable age and size. There was a long drive to the next garden, near Littlehampton, Berri Court. We were received by the owner, Mr Turner, who showed us round an interesting garden, surrounded by, but well sheltered from, neighbours. Again this was a compartment garden, each area being shut off by a hedge or flint wall and complete in itself. There was a great diversity of plants, but no rhododendrons or camellias and therefore of little special relevance to us. The owner was enthusiastic, knowledgeable and friendly. He showed us a good white *Abutilon, Drimys winteri, Olearia scilloniensis, Eucalyptus nitens, Teucrium, Fejoa, Myrtus luma, Zelkova*, various phormiums, *Viburnum macrocephalum* with large lacecap sterile florets, *V. betulifolium* bearing in autumn swaying branches with bunches of red currant-like fruits, as well as a nice *Abies koreana* and another *Pinus montezumae.*

Our next day's visit was to Wakehurst Place, leased by the Royal Botanic Gardens Kew from the National Trust. Here we had the good fortune to have our Chairman, John Bond, who has an intimate knowledge of the whole complex and, indeed, each individual plant because of his friendship with Tony Schilling, until recently the Keeper of the woody and shrubby plants. The garden was originally laid out by Gerald Loder, later Lord Wakehurst, one of the founding members of the Rhododendron Society formed in 1915 by the small group of enthusiasts who helped to fund 'Chinese' Wilson, George Forrest and Frank Kingdon Ward. In addition he was a member of the extensive Loder family who owned several influential gardens in this part of the Sussex Weald. The natural lie of the land, heavily wooded, dissected by deep combes and well watered with springs lends itself to imaginative planting, and throughout its occupation by Lord Wakehurst, Sir Henry Price and Kew, the

garden has been the centre of innovative recreation of the Sino-Himalayas. Apart from Reg Wallace, Sir Henry's gardener, Kew's takeover brought in its Directors, Sir George Taylor and later Ian (Sir Ghillean) Prance, and, more intimately Tony Schilling whose Himalayan experience and personal touch has created, in spite of the devastation caused by the great storms, a scene as near to its original surroundings as could be imagined in the Home Counties. One of the features that makes the Weald so particularly valuable horticulturally is its local climate – it is both high and warm. In John's telling phrase, while you wear an overcoat at Kew, at Wakehurst you wear a jacket. The two areas simulating the Sino-Himalayan scene are the Asian Heath Garden and the Himalayan Glade, and it was through these two that John led us, pointing out notable plants on the way and explaining that in the high altitudes the 'heath', exposed to searing winds but protected in winter by deep snow, is home to the various dwarf rhododendrons and their companion plants, many of which do so well in Britain. The Himalayan Glade occupying a deep valley perhaps conjures up more successfully a vision of the great temperate forests where the larger and more tender rhododendrons grow. It was an apt lesson to walk there with John Bond and we profited by it.

Before our visit to Borde Hill, another of the Wealden gardens made famous by the early members of the Rhododendron Association, we visited Duckyls, Lady Taylor's garden which has what must surely be the most breathtaking view of the Weald between the North and South Downs to be seen anywhere. This garden has an extensive wild hillside well planted with rhododendrons, camellias and magnolias, that are now of some maturity and it was a pleasure to wander round while noting them.

Borde Hill which suffered a temporary decline after the death of Robert Stephenson Clarke (grandson of Col Robert the first owner) and from the great storm, has now charitable status and has recently received a Heritage Lottery Grant to refurbish the basic structure of paths and walls. The fourth generation of the family, Andrewjohn, is an active trustee. Our young lady guide, Maggie Lamb, was knowledgeable and enthusiastic and pointed out how the grant is making a substantial difference to the appearance of the garden including several new features. Many of the older plants and trees are still to be seen, notably magnolias (*Magnolia campbellii*, *M. sargentiana* var. *robusta*, *M.* × *veitchii*, *M. fraseri* and *M. hypoleuca*, both the last in flower, as well as *M. sprengeri* var. *diva*), and the original *Camellia williamsii* 'Donation' bred here by Col Robert and his gardener, Jack Vass. We walked through the Old Rhododendron Garden as it was in its heyday, the Azalea Ring, the Garden of Allah and the Long Walk designed and planted by Jack Vass, and some of us were pleased to see the statue of the veiled lady – 'The Bride' – such a feature of the garden. We were all sorry there was no time for an extended visit to Warren and Gore Woods where so many of the most varied and interesting rhododendron species raised from seed sent back by the 'Great Collectors' are planted. But that must be for next time.

On our last morning, before we all separated, we visited a small and very secluded private garden belonging to Dr and Mrs Steven Smith at 'Moorlands' near Crowborough. This is an old farmhouse, deep in Ashdown Forest, hidden in a valley through which a tributary (no name!) of the Medway flows. The steep sides of the valley upon which the farmhouse stands are terraced now on three levels. The garden has been created within the last 50 years by two generations of loving owners. It is imaginatively planted with a list in the informative leaflet too long to quote here, but enough to make one wish to see it in other seasons. There is a small hot and dry area as a contrast to the prevailing feeling of damp woodland. Trees are many and various and those we picked out were *Camellia* 'Cornish Snow', *Nothofagus antarctica*, *Arbutus unedo*, a cut-leaved Alder (*Alnus glutinosa* 'Imperialis'), *Metasequoia glyptostroboides* with a fascinating trunk full of holes, *Pinus patula* and a yew covered in *Tropaeolum speciosum*. Rhododendrons included the marmalade-coloured *R. dichroanthum* subsp. *scyphocalyx* and *R. fictolacteum*. The bank opposite the house had been planted for autumn colour. What more can one say, except that the owners were most hospitable, true plant lovers and sent us on our homeward way tanked up with hot coffee and horticultural gossip.

For the first time this tour was organized by a travel firm specialising in garden tours. Boxwood Tours were responsible for choosing the gardens we visited and dealing directly with the garden owners, for arranging accommodation in Crowborough and transport by private coach. Although different from the tours hitherto arranged by the Group itself, the general consensus of those taking part was that we saw a good mix of private gardens and those open to the public, though perhaps the choice did not always sufficiently allow for our specialised interests. We benefited at all the gardens from the knowledge of those who showed us round.

Cynthia Postan was for 10 years the Honorary Editor of the Year Book and also of the 1996 publication *The Rhododendron Story*

The Rhododendron and Camellia Competitions

Early Rhododendron Competition
16–17 March, 1999

At long last it is pleasing to report a much greater support for the Early Rhododendron Competition than in the past decade with the 82 entries being twice the number exhibited in 1998. It is also pleasing to report keen competition in many of the classes with the judges really having to earn their free lunch – a change from several past years! This improvement was largely due to the three big gardens, that in the past have supported the early show intermittently, all coinciding in the same year. There was a welcome display of entries of section Vireya in the classes for plants grown under glass which gave little chance to the entries of those from the other sections more often seen, e.g. Maddenia. If this pattern is continued in future years, a case could be made for an additional class solely for Vireyas and their hybrids perhaps.

Class 1 for three species – won by the City of Swansea, Clyne Gardens with trusses of *R. macabeanum* KW7724, *R. meddianum* and *R. falconeri* subsp. *eximium*. Second prize to Nymans (National Trust) with *R. oreodoxa* var. *fargesii*, *R. uvarifolium*, *R. oreodoxa* var. *oreodoxa*. Third prize to Exbury who showed a lovely blood red *R. arboreum*, *R. macabeanum* and *R. calophytum*.

Class 2 for a spray of a species, was won by Nymans with *R. oreodoxa* var. *oreodoxa*. Second prize to Exbury with *R. racemosum* and third prize to Swansea with *R. falconeri* subsp. *eximium*.

Class 3 for one truss of a species had five entries dominated by the *R. macabeanum* KW7724 which has so graced this early show in recent years (photograph of which was on the front cover of the 1998 Year Book). Swansea's and Nymans' exhibits of this species won the first and second prizes respectively with Swansea also winning the third prize with a fine *R. arboreum* var. *roseum*.

Class 4 for one truss of a species in subsects. Arborea or Argyrophylla was won by Swansea with *R. arboreum* var. *roseum*. Exbury were second with the same species but of a much deeper pink and Nymans had a fine truss of *R. lanigerum* for third prize.

Class 5 was the only class in which a first prize was not awarded. It calls for a truss from subsects. Barbata, Glischra or Maculifera and Swansea showed *R. strigillosum* for second prize with Nymans gaining third for their *R. glischrum* subsp. *glischroides* F26448.

Class 6 for a truss of a species in the Grandia or Falconera sections gave Nymans just revenge over Swansea from class 3. Here their *R. macabeanum* KW77 gained first prize with Swansea's truss of the same species only awarded third. Swansea did win second with a truss of *R. falconeri* subsp. *eximium*.

Class 7 for a truss from subsect. Fortunea saw Nymans winning all three prizes. Their first prize entry showed a new form of *R. calophytum*; collected by Keith Rushforth under his collection No. 141. Their two variants of *R. oreodoxa* gained second and third.

Class 8 for subsect. Neriiflora had but

one entry – this from Nymans with a truss of *R. piercei* gaining first prize.

Class 9 for a truss from subsects. Campylocarpa, Selensia, Thomsonia or Williamsiana saw Nymans winning the two prizes awarded. First went to *R. hylaeum* and second to *R. campylocarpum*.

Class 10 for a spray from a host of 16 subsects. again saw Nymans gaining all three prizes. First went to their *R. siderophyllum* (of subsect. Triflora) with second and third going to different forms of *R. racemosum* (sect. Scabrifolia).

Class 11 for a truss from any other section not mentioned in the foregoing classes of species had by far the greatest number of entries for any class – 11 in total, mostly from Nymans who deservedly won all four prizes (in order) with *R. uvarifolium, R. fulvum* F24110, *R. wasonii* and *R. principis*. Other species shown and rarely seen at shows were *R. anthosphaerum, R. adenogynum, R. tanastylum*, and a splendid form of *R. irroratum* from Exbury with delicate markings in the throats of each flower.

Class 12 for a spray from any section, as in Class 11 had but one entry, this from Swansea with *R. irroratum* for the first prize.

Class 13, one truss each of three hybrids in each entry and was won by Exbury with 'Shilsonii', 'Androcles' and 'Our Kate' (see Fig. 26). Swansea gained the other two prizes with 'Cornubia', 'Janet' and 'Pink Delight' for second and Media grex, *R. sutchuenense × R. niveum*, *R.* 'Chrysomanicum', for third.

Class 14 for a spray of any hybrid had two entries, both of 'Cilpinense' with first prize going to Nymans for a superb spray of this delightful early flowerer and second prize to Exbury.

Class 15 for one truss of any hybrid was won by Nymans with 'Shilsonii', they also gained second with 'Nobleanum Album'

while Exbury won third with 'Androcles'.

Class 16 for a truss of a hybrid in which one parent must be a species from a list shown on the Show Schedule had Exbury winning first prize with 'Werei', while Swansea gained second and third with 'Ivery's Scarlet' and 'Glory of Penjerrick'.

Class 17 for a truss of a hybrid in which one parent is a species of subsect. Fortunea had two entries only. Exbury won first prize with 'Androcles', while Swansea took second with 'Giraldii' which used to have its own species status as a variant of *R. sutchuenense*.

Class 18 for a truss of a hybrid in which neither parent is a species from a list shown on the Show Schedule, gave Swansea the chance to show off more of their Grandia hybrids which have dominated this class in recent years. First prize was awarded for *R. grande × R. macabeanum* and the second for *R. macabeanum × R. hodgsonii*, which had the flowers of the former with the foliage of the latter – a truly splendid hybrid having the best of both parents.

Class 19 for a truss of any elepidote hybrid not allowed for in foregoing classes, had a Vireya hybrid 'Just Peachy' gaining the only prize for Mr C Fairweather who in recent years has been establishing a collection of Vireya rhododendrons and now runs a nursery for these increasing-in-popularity greenhouse plants.

There were no entries for Class 20.

Class 21 for a tender species or hybrid grown under glass, one truss, had a plethora of Vireya flowers – a very colourful sight and displaying the great range of flower form and colour available to interest and attract spectators new to this section. Mr C Fairweather won first and second prizes with 'Cameo Spico' and 'Pink Delight' with Dr R Jack winning third with the species *R. christianae*.

Class 22 is for a spray of a tender plant

with the same description as for class 21. Here again there was a very colourful display with Mr C Fairweather winning all the prizes with his Vireyas. First prize to 'First Light', second to 'Rosie Posie' and third to 'Little Pinkie'.

Finally, mention should be made to an exhibit in Class 21, shown by Dr R Jack of *R. seinghkuense* KW9254 which was completely swamped and overshadowed by all the Vireyas in this class. It is a plant discovered by Frank Kingdon Ward in Burma, a member of subsect. Edgeworthia, with very large bright yellow flowers in comparison to the leaf size. Although exhibits of this species have been shown before by other exhibitors at this show, it is very rare in cultivation. It is encouraging to know that it has not been lost.

David Farnes

The Main Rhododendron Competition 27–28 April, 1999 – Species

Frost two weeks before the show was not a good omen, however, everyone was pleasantly surprised to find a show which was an improvement upon last year that was well supported.

Our thanks to all those who do keep the rhododendron in front of the public. Is it not a pity, that more nurserymen do not exhibit in the competition when perhaps in the long run it may be to their advantage?

Class 1, six species, one truss of each. Sadly only one entry from Exbury Garden, worthy of the Lionel de Rothschild Challenge Cup – the six fine trusses being *R. fulvum, R. campanulatum, R. niveum, R. coriaceum, R. arizelum* and *R. fictolacteum*.

Class 2, three species, one truss of each. First prize, a near perfect *R. roxieanum, R. glaucophyllum* and *R. aberconwayi* from Mr Gilbert of Cornwall. Second prize, Exbury's

R. orbiculare, R. thomsonii and *R. smirnowii*.

Class 3, any species, one truss. A well supported class, which no doubt gave the judges a challenge. First prize and the Mclaren Challenge Cup went to a superb *R. argyrophyllum* 'Chinese Silver' (see Fig. 27) from Brian Wright of Crowborough. Second and third prizes were close, but Exbury's *R. hodgsonii* 'Poet's Lawn' pipped Isabella Plantation with a rather pale coloured *R. wightii*.

Class 4, any species, one spray. The one entry, from Exbury, was a colourful and well staged exhibit of *R. davidsonianum* also gaining the Roza Stevenson Challenge Cup, a repeat of last year.

Class 5, any species of subsect. Arborea or subsect. Argyrophylla, one truss. A perfect *R. niveum* gained the first prize for Exbury but there were no other entries.

Class 6, any species of subsect. Barbata, subsect. Glischra or subsect. Maculifera, one truss. The judges awarded a third prize to a slightly marked *R. anwheiense*, the only entry, from Exbury.

Class 7, a species of subsect Campanulata, subsect Fulgensia or subsect. Lanata, one truss. A truss of *R. campanulatum* from Exbury, the only entry, received first prize.

Class 8, a species of subsect. Grandia or subsect. Falconera, one truss. A good *R. fictolacteum* which deserved stronger competition was placed first.

Class 9, any species of subsect. Fortunea, one truss. A new and most welcome exhibitor from Plymouth, Mr J Bodenham took the honours in a well contested class, gaining first prize with a lovely *R. decorum* and third prize with *R. griffithianum*. Exbury gained second prize with *R. orbiculare*.

Class 10, any species of subsect. Fulva, subsect. Irrorata or subsect. Parishia, one truss. A *R. fulvum* well worthy of First Prize shown by Exbury was the only entry.

Class 11, any species of subsect. Taliensia, one truss. A well shaped, clean truss of *R. roxieanum* won first prize for Exbury. Very close, in second place was a very good *R. sphaeroblastum*, all the way from Scotland shown by Dr Jack. Mr Bodenham's *R. faberi* gained third prize.

Class 12, any species of subsect. Neriiflora, one spray. Much interest was shown in the only entry shown as *R. haematodes*. The decision of the judges was that it was NAS.

Class 13, any species of Pontica, one truss. Dr Jack reversed the order of Class 11 by beating Exbury to first prize with a near perfect *R. caucasicum* and they were second with *R. metternichii*.

Class 14, any species of subsect. Thomsonia, subsect. Selensia or subsect. Campylocarpa, one spray. Surprisingly only one entry, *R. thomsonii* from Exbury.

Class 18, any species of subsect. Edgeworthia or subsect. Maddenia, one spray. No first prize awarded. Dr Dayton gained the second prize with his *R. cubittii* in front of Exbury's rather young *R. burmanicum*.

Class 19, any species of subsect. Maddenia (Dalhousiae Alliance and Megacalyx Alliance only) one truss. First prize went to Exbury with *R. johnstonianum*, no second prize was awarded and third prize went to Dr Dayton with *R. cubittii*.

Class 20, any species of subsect. Triflora and subsect. Heliolepida other than *R. augustinii*, one spray. A fresh and clean vase of *R. rubiginosum* gained the only prize – a first for Exbury.

Class 21, *R. augustinii*, one spray. Not for the first time Exbury received the first prize in this class with a lovely exhibit of a very good form of this species.

Class 22, any species of subsect. Cinnabarina, subsect. Tephropepla or subsect. Virgata, one spray. Exbury's vase of *R. cinnabarinum* with very clean foliage was rightly awarded first prize.

Class 23, any species of subsect. Campylogyna, subsect. Genestieriana or subsect. Glauca, one spray. Once again Exbury was the only exhibitor, with a large spray of *R. glaucophyllum* winning first prize.

Class 24, any species of subsect. Lapponica, one spray. Dr Jack provided the two entries, his *R rupicola* was second to his *R. hippophaeoides*, both in very good form.

Class 27, any species of sect. Pogonanthum or subsect. Lepidota, one spray. Mr Gilbert, with the only entry, showed *R. baileyi* (see front cover) to win a good first.

Class 29, any species of sect. Vireya, one truss. This class demanded close attention from enthusiasts, and what pleasure to see these gems of the genus! Mr Bodenham was awarded first prize with *R. himantodes*, and also second prize for *R. nervulosum*. Mr Fairweather of Beaulieu made it a close contest with his *R. jasminiflorum* in third place and gained a worthy fourth with *R. loranthiflorum*. May we hope that both these exhibitors will return next year with these Vireyas to promote them.

Class 30, any species of deciduous Azalea, one spray. First prize to Exbury with *R. rhombicum* (syn. *reticulata*).

Class 31, any species of evergreen azalea, one spray. A lovely vase, in tip-top condition of *R. amoenum* gained first prize for Exbury.

Before closing these notes, mention must be made of three exhibits not in the competition. First, the collection of *R. sinogrande* × *R. falconeri* hybrids staged by Exbury, with 'Fortune' as the centre-piece, this also included 'Stanley', 'Ottawa' a quite superb 'Churchill' and 'Montreal'.

Matthewman of Pontefract had a pleasing stand of mostly dwarf rhododendrons including 'Ginny Gee', 'Merganiser', the charming 'Egret' and the very healthy looking 'Ruby Hart'.

Last, but no means least, the finest exhibit of rhododendron hybrids seen at Westminster or anywhere else for many years was from Slocock Knaphill Nursery. It was a beautifully staged exhibit which brought back memories of times past, with such first class plants as 'Doncaster', 'Countess of Athlone', 'Fastuosum Flore-Pleno', 'Souvenire de Dr Endtz', 'Mrs G W Leak' and 'Mrs Furnival' (and her daughter).

A special thanks to these exhibitors.

Archie Skinner

The Main Rhododendron Competition 27–28 April, 1999 – Hybrids

First came spring. It was so early and so assuringly mild that plants I had, in previous years, persuaded, cajoled and threatened to bloom in time for this event looked like being over and done with before a vase was staged. Could it be that I would be left with only a few precocious hardy hybrids to display? Not a bit of it, because then, in mid-April, came winter. It brought snow, hail, gales, floods and devastating frosts which in the South-East lasted several consecutive nights at temperatures that dropped to well below zero.

Needless to say, much of the early flower was dismally turned to pulp while the rest was stopped, almost dead, in its tracks. But nature is a wonderful, if infuriating, force and a week after all had calmed down one could see that there would be at least one or two good things to harvest for the show bench. Indeed, the hybrid classes produced 83 staged entries, the largest contingent of exhibits for some years.

Class 32 for six trusses saw just one entry from Exbury Gardens. Under the stewardship of Mr Edmund de Rothschild

and head gardener Mr Paul Martin, they were deservedly awarded first prize with a highly colourful grouping of 'Calfort Bounty', 'Hawk Crest', 'Susan', 'Queen of Hearts', 'Loderi Venus' and 'Roza Stevenson'.

Class 33 for three trusses attracted four entries and was well won by The Isabella Plantation, Richmond Park, Surrey. They showed 'Beauty of Littleworth', 'Queen of Hearts', and 'Loders White'. Second was Brian Wright from Crowborough, Sussex with 'W.F.H.', 'Lamellen' and an un-named *R. orbiculare* hybrid.

Class 34, one truss for The Loder Cup was won by Brian Wright with the bright scarlet *R. haematodes* cross 'W.F.H'. As if signalling his determination to claim the trophy, he also took second and third prizes with 'Lamellen' and 'Roza Stevenson'.

Class 35, one spray, saw first prize awarded to Exbury with 'Vienna'. This is a worthy and similar sibling to their other fine creation, 'Idealist'. Second was Dr. John Dayton of Dorking, Surrey, with 'White Wings', a somewhat surprising entry to see in this class since, as a 'tender' in the South, it would normally be grown under glass.

Class 36 for three trusses of plants bred and raised in the garden of the exhibitor was won by Exbury. They showed 'Jessica de Rothschild', 'Hermione Knight', and that well-known, wine red, 'Queen of Hearts' – a pretty trio that won them The Crossfield Challenge Cup.

Class 37 for a single truss of Loderi group cultivars saw only two prizes being awarded. First went to Exbury for the good shell-pink 'Loderi Sir Joseph Hooker'. Second went to Brian Wright for 'Loderi King George'.

Class 38 for one truss of any hybrid of which one parent is of subsect. Fortunea.

This was won by Mr John Bodenham of Plymouth, Devon, for the fragrant and very showy 'Cornish Cross'. Second was Exbury's 'Calfort Bounty' and third Brian Wright's 'Lamellen'.

Class 39 for one spray of a *R. williamsianum* parent. Exbury were the only entrants in this class. They showed 'Bow Bells' which although not fully open still persuaded the judges that it was worth a first prize.

Class 40 for one truss of subsect. Campylocarpa hybrids. Although Brian Wright was awarded first, second and third prizes in this class, it was only his winning entry, 'Roza Stevenson' that merited a prize at all. His runner-up, 'Carita Inchmery' was, in fact, 'Naomi Nautilus' which should have been given N.A.S. since it is of *R. fortunei* descent. His third placed truss was just as inappropriate as it was labelled '*R. orbiculare* hybrid' which does not have a lot to do with subsect. Campylocarpa. Not only a clear lapse of concentration but a clear lapse of judging.

Class 41 was for one truss of subsect. Neriiflora hybrids. Although this was a nice example of family hybridisation – two Lionel de Rothschild creations ('Karkov' and 'Gipsy King') crossed by Edmund de Rothschild to produce 'David Rockefeller' – it was not strictly as schedule, as the Class asked for one parent to be of subsect. Neriiflora. The second placed entry, 'May Day' entered by John Bodenham was perfectly in order and should have been given first prize.

Class 42 for one truss of *R. thomsonii* hybrids. No prizes were awarded, although the only entry, 'Luscombei' did receive a Commended for Exbury.

Class 43 for one truss of subsect. Grandia or Falconera hybrids was won by Exbury with a symmetrically neat truss of the mauve flowered 'Colonel Rogers'.

Class 44 for one truss of *R. griersonianum* hybrids attracted only one entry again, the fiery red 'Matador' from Exbury. It was properly awarded first prize.

Class 45 for one truss of subsect. Taliensia hybrids was easily won by Exbury with their fine yellow hybrid 'Mariloo'. Trailing in it's wake were the two entries of *R. roxieanum* hybrid, 'Blewbury'. The better of these came from R Gilbert who gained second prize and the lesser from Brian Wright who took third.

Class 46 for one truss of any subsect. Pontica hybrid. There were two entries, both from Exbury. First was 'Hermione Knight', a strong, handsome pink and second 'Seven Stars', the *R. yakushimanum* hybrid.

Class 47 for one truss of subsect. Arborea or Argyrophylla hybrids. Although Exbury's 'Colonel Rogers' was the only contestant in this class, it could muster no more than a second prize.

Class 48 for one spray of subsect. Cinnabarina hybrids. Again it was left to Exbury to provide the sole entry. This time it was the attractive 'Biskra', yet another of their famous hybrids, which took first prize.

Class 49 for one truss of subsect. Maddenia or Edgworthia hybrids. Although this class can be one of the most attractive in the competition, this year the exhibits, and there were eight, did look a little tired. But fresh enough to win was Exbury's un-named *R. tyermannii* cross with Dr Robbie Jack's good 'Fragrantissimum' in second place and Mr R Gilbert's 'Lady Alice Fitzwilliam' × *R. edgworthii* in third.

Class 50 for one spray of subsect. Triflora hybrids. Exbury once more provided the only entry with the brilliant blue 'St Tudy' which was duly awarded first prize.

Class 51 for one truss of any lepidote

Fig. 22: The winner of the Photographic Competition, R. niveum *'Crown Equerry' taken by Mr J D Bottle (see p.52)*

Fig. 23: Second in the Photographic Competition, Magnolia *'Greta Eisenhut' taken by M J-P Chatelard at P van Veen's garden in Switzerland (see p.52)*

Fig. 24: Third equal in the Photographic competition , R. taggianum 'Harry Tagg' taken by Dr G Hargreaves at Arduaine, Argyll (see p.52)

Fig. 25: Third equal in the Photographic Competition, R bureavii taken by Mr J D Bottle (see p.52)

Fig. 26: R. *'Our Kate' exhibited by Exbury at the 1999 Early Rhododendron competition (see p.68)*

Fig. 27: R. argyrophyllum *'Chinese Silver' winner of the McClaren Cup (see p.69)*

Fig. 28: Camellia *'Janet Waterhouse' exhibited by Anne Hooton at the 1999 Main Camellia Competition*

Fig. 29: C. *'Julia Hamiter' a first prize winner for Ann Hooton at the Main Camellia Competition (see p.77)*

(Bc)

Fig. 30: C. 'Augusto Pinto' at the 1999 Main Camellia Competition (see p.75)

Fig. 31: C. 'Mrs D.W. Davies', an entry in the single flowered C. × williamsii cultivar class (see p.77)

Fig. 32: Rhododendron *'New Comet'* × R. caloxanthum, *a cross made in 1984 at Silverwell , Berwickshire, Scotland (see p.52)*

hybrid not allowed for in the earlier classes saw only one entry, 'Dora Amateis', which, looking quite insignificant and somewhat embarrassed, was rather generously awarded third prize. Perhaps here, one ought to state that lepidotes will hardly provide a decent showbench truss which calls into question the wisdom of including this class in the competition schedule at all.

Class 52 for any other lepidote sprays was a totally different matter. Here 'Dora Amateis', shown as a spray by Exbury was completely vindicated and came into its own to win first prize.

Class 53 for one truss of any elepidote hybrid not allowed for in earlier classes was won by the Knap Hill hybrid 'Furnival's Daughter' entered by John Bodenham. I must say that it is always interesting to see these hardy plants exhibited so early in the season. Second and third prizes went to Brian Wright for the American hybrid 'Half-dan Lem' and an un-named *R. campanulatum* hybrid.

Class 54 for any other elepidote sprays attracted only one entry, a very striking 'Queen of Hearts' from Exbury (see Fig. 14). It was one of Lionel de Rothschild's last crosses and was awarded yet another of the first prizes it must have won over the years.

Class 55 for one truss of any hybrid grown under glass was not so much a class but more of a promotional statement for vireyas – and how effective it was. Altogether there were 15 exhibits, 12 of which were Vireyas, making it the best supported class in the competition. The standard was so high that the judges had an extremely difficult job in selecting prize winners. First was given to John Boddenham with the richly exuberant *R. aurigeranum* × 'Pink Delight'. Second to Fairweather's Garden Centre, Beaulieu with the aptly named 'Shantung

Rose' – long, slim, perfumed corollas in shades of yellow, orange and vermilion, enticing in every way. Third to Exbury with their earlier exhibited exotic *R. tyermannii* hybrid. A fourth was given to John Bodenham for 'Bob's Choice' a quite disarming pink bloom. Mr. Bodenham also received a Highly Commended award for 'Tropical Fanfare' and a Commended award for *R. laetum* × *R. javanicum*.

Class 56 for one spray of any other hybrid grown under glass attracted one exhibit, 'Rubicon', entered by Dr. John Dayton. This is an interesting New Zealand hybrid that one would not expect to be grown under glass since it's parents are 'Noyo Chief' (at one time thought to be a form of *R. kingianum*) and 'Kilimanjaro' the Exbury hybrid. It was surprisingly awarded a third prize.

Class 57 for one spray of any evergreen azalea was well won by Exbury showing a fine 'Hinodegiri'. Second and third was The Isabella Plantation who presented good exhibits of the creamy-white, hose-in-hose 'Shin-seikai' and 'Orange Beauty'.

Class 58 for one spray of any deciduous azalea was one by Exbury with 'Duchess of Kent', a most impressive yellow. Second was Brian Wright with the orange 'Floradora'.

Apart from the competition itself, it must be mentioned that Exbury Gardens put on a fine display of their famous 'Fortune' hybrid. There were several different blooms, all impressive, from the same *R. falconeri* and *R. sinogrande* cross made by Lionel de Rothschild in the late 1920s. To describe the blooms simply as 'yellow' would not do them justice, although it should be pointed out that an outstandingly clear yellow received an FCC in 1938. Subsequently other plants from the same cross have flowered. The results of the 'Fortune' grex can be seen today in The Winter Gardens at Exbury in Hampshire.

Of the many good trade stands, it must be recorded that Slococks of Woking, Surrey mounted a truly brilliant display of hardy hybrids. The colours, if you like them bold, were outstanding and the condition of both the blooms and the foliage was excellent. Congratulations must go to all those involved for not only creating a superb, gold medal stand on the day but also for their painstaking and skilful pre-show efforts in advancing the flowers to a peak at precisely the right time. Indeed, it was a delight to see, in April, old favourites that you would not normally expect to see on display until Chelsea e.g. Mrs. Furnival, Old Port, Lavender Girl, Ripe Corn, Gomer Waterer, etc.

Brian Wright

The Early Camellia Competition
16–17 March, 1999

The season was remarkable for wet, warm weather – much to the liking of camellias – and the quality of the blossoms on show was generally very high. Up to this show, there had been little frost. The entries in some classes were up, and the whole created a beautiful display.

Class 10, any three single-flowered cultivars, one bloom of each, had a delightful bloom in the entry of D R Strauss, who took first place with 'Furo-An', 'Rosetsu' and 'Clarissa', a very pretty, well-formed bloom in a sharp pink with deeper pink stripes. Edmund de Rothschild took second and Mrs Petherick third.

Class 13 attracted 19 entries, and D R Strauss took first with 'Wildfire' – a superb bright red bloom which shines. Chatsworth House Trust took second with 'Drama Girl' and A W Simons third with 'Haku Rakuten'.

Class 14, with 20 entries each requiring three blooms, was spectacular, especially the entry from Chatsworth House Trust showing 'Dixie Knight', 'Kramer's Supreme' and 'Premier', all rich red, making a wonderful display. Mrs Petherick took first with 'Dona Herzilia de Freitas Magalhaes', 'Mathotiana Supreme' and 'Kramer's Supreme'. D R Strauss was third with 'Emperor of Russia', 'Faith' and 'Kramer's Supreme'.

Class 17 for rose-formed or formal double cultivars had 19 entries. First, Mrs Petherick with 'Joshua Youtz'; second Mrs Betterley with 'Augusto L'Gouveia Pinto', a cultivar which has figured largely in the show some years, but while its popularity has waned its beauty certainly has not, and the strong lavender flush over pink gives it an aura quite unmistakeable. A W Simons exhibited an unknown bloom for third, and D R Strauss 'Julia Drayton' for fourth.

Class 18 attracted 12 entries, but each was of six cultivars, one bloom of each. It was won by Mr Edmund de Rothschild, whose entry included three cultivars not often shown: 'Madge Miller', 'Cameo' and 'Strawberry Parfait'.

Class 19 was favoured with 39 exceptional flowers. The judges awarded first, second and third, also fourth highly commended and commended. Out of 13 entries of three blooms each, David Davis took first with 'Powder Puff', 'Carter's Sunburst' and 'Tiffany', a superb entry. Second came Mrs Petherick with 'Jessica Kaby', 'Haku Rakuten' and 'Grand Slam'. Third Chatsworth House Trust, showing 'Dr Tinsley', 'Serenade' and 'Leonora Novick'. Fourth D R Strauss, with 'Clarissa', 'C M Wilson' and 'Adolphe Audusson'. Highly commended, D R Strauss with 'Margaret Rose', 'Lady Lock' and 'Wildlife'. Commended, D R Strauss with 'Cheryl Lynn', 'Cardinal Variegated' and 'Berenice Perfection'.

Class 21 demanded a *C. reticulata* hybrid of which one parent is *C. × williamsii* or *C. saluenensis*. There were nine entries. Chatsworth House Trust came first with a superb bloom of 'Francie L', A W Simons second with 'Valley Knudson', third, Mrs Petherwick with another beautiful 'Francie L' bloom and fourth Chatsworth House Trust with 'Leonard Messel'. Highly commended was D R Strauss, who showed a bloom of 'Inspiration'.

Class 24, for any single *C. × williamsii*, was particularly notable for the entry of Chatsworth House Trust. In judging it came fourth, but 'Ruby Bells' is a delightful cultivar which stands out. First came Ann Hooton with 'Mary Larcom', second, D R Strauss with 'Mary Jobson', third, D R Strauss with 'Elizabeth de Rothschild'.

The *C. × williamsii* entries in Classes 24 and 25 were quite beautiful, and it could not have been easy to select an order of merit.

Class 27, which called for a hybrid other than *C. reticulata* or *C. × williamsii*, produced seven entries. First, D R Strauss, with 'Taro Kaya', second David Davis with 'Nicky Crisp', third, A W Simons with 'Quintesscience'.

Class 28 was for any yellow species or hybrid. For this there is no great choice, but there were 10 entries. First, D R Strauss with 'Brushfield's Yellow', second, Mr Betterley with 'Jury's Yellow', and third, A W Simons with 'Brushfield's Yellow'. How long will it be before the strong yellow colours of the *C. chrysantha* species brighten up this class?

Finally, class 29, which gives a chance to an exhibitor who has not won a first prize in a previous RHS Camellia Competition. Lady Boyd came first with a lovely bloom of 'Mandalay Queen'. May this give her the inspiration to put in more blooms in the coming competitions.

Overall honours are between D R Strauss, who was awarded six firsts, and Chatsworth House Trust, who were awarded five firsts, but 12 competitors had their blooms placed in various classes and great credit is due to them.

The Main Camellia Competition 13–14 April, 1999

The 13 and 14 April 1999 followed the Early Competition by a short four weeks, but in that period the weather had completely changed and some severe frosts took a heavy toll of blossoms in some parts of the country. However, a beautiful display was mounted with a wide variety of cultivars represented.

Class 10. At this show, pride of place must go to the entries for the Leonardslee Bowl. To produce 12 different blooms is a challenge, yet nine competitors took it up. Edmund de Rothschild richly deserved his first place, showing 'Augusto Pinto' (see Fig. 30), a superb flower with a lovely lilac sheen, 'Kramer's Supreme', 'Margaret Davis', 'Tomorrow', 'Nuccio's Pearl', 'Pope John', 'Mary Taylor', 'Elsie Jury', 'Tiffany', 'Anticipation' and 'Drama Girl'. Second was Ann Hooton, who showed 'Rubescens', 'Nuccio's Jewel', 'Satan's Robe', 'Mona Jury', 'Grand Prix', 'Wilber Foss', 'Matterhorn', 'R. L. Wheeler', 'Julia Hamiter', 'Miss Tulare', 'Royalty' and 'Dr Clifford Parks'. Third was A W Simon, showing 'Anticipation', 'Souzas Pavlova', a lovely cultivar with a delightful scent, 'Hilda Jamieson', 'Annabel Lansdell', 'Elsie Jury', 'Augusto Pinto', 'Desire', 'Inspiration', 'Debbie', 'R. L. Wheeler', 'Otto Hopfer' and 'Lily Pons'. Fourth was David Davis with 'Diana's Charm', 'Tiffany', 'Annie Wylam', 'Nuccio's Jewel', 'Nuccio's Gem', 'Nuccio's Pearl', 'Matterhorn', 'Senorita',

'Swan Lake', 'Guilio Nuccio', 'Primavera' and 'C. M. Hovey'. Highly commended was D R Strauss showing 'Lavinia', 'Maggi', 'Rosea', 'Dr Burnside Variegated', 'Elegans Splendor', 'Adolphe Audusson', 'Charlean', 'Hawaii', 'Elegans', 'Faith', 'Extravaganza' and 'Mrs D. W. Davis' (see Fig. 31).

Class 11 asked for only six blooms from the competitors, and there were eight entries. Mr A W Simons came first with 'Wilamina', 'Night Rider', 'Little Bit', 'Sir Victor Davis', 'Tom Thumb' and 'Burgundy Gem'. All these are cultivars with small flowers, and it was a most imaginative entry.

Classes 12 and 13 were devoted to single camellia cultivars. Class 12 attracted four entries. Edmund de Rothschild came first with 'Diatorin', 'Red Cardinal' and 'Jupiter', and third with 'Japonica Bonetsu', 'Red Cardinal' and 'Hatsu Sakura', while Ann Hooton took second place with 'Jennifer Turnbull', 'Henry Turnbull' and 'Juno'. Class 13 attracted 9 entries and demanded only one bloom. Edmund de Rothschild came first with 'Red Cardinal'. Second was D R Strauss with 'Clarissa', third, D R Strauss with 'Alba Simplex' and fourth D R Strauss with 'Evelyn'. Highly commended was Josephine Newman with 'Adelina Patti'.

Classes 14 and 15 were for semi-double cultivars of *Camellia japonica*, and some of the most beautiful blooms come under this heading. There were seven entries in class 14, each entry requiring three blooms. Ann Hooton came first with 'Bob Hope', 'Elizabeth Dowd' and 'Grand Prix'. Second was D R Strauss with 'Adolphe Audusson', 'Guilio Nuccio', and 'Drama Girl' and third, Edmund de Rothschild with 'Drama Girl', 'Waterloo' and 'R. L. Wheeler'. Class 15 attracted 12 entries. First was Edmund de Rothschild with 'Kelvingtonia', second, Josephine Newman showing 'Lady Clare',

third, D R Strauss with 'Wildfire' and fourth, Ann Hooton with a beautiful bloom with no recorded name.

Class 16 for anemone and peony-formed cultivars of *C. japonica*: Edmund de Rothschild came first and his entry of three cultivars was brightened by a superb bloom of 'Kramer's Supreme'. His other two were 'Elegans Champagne' and 'Barbara Mary'. Second, David Davis, showed 'Nuccio's Jewel', 'Annie Wylam' and 'Onetia Holland'. D R Strauss was third with 'Hanatachi Bama', 'Elegans Splendor' and 'Midnight' and fourth with 'Hawaii', 'Extravaganza' and 'Faith'. A W Simons was highly commended for his entry of 'Margaret Davis', 'Kramer's Supreme' and 'Owen Henry'.

Class 17: there were 11 entries. First place went to Ann Hooton with her entry of a bloom of 'R. L. Wheeler', second, a bloom of 'Nuccio's Jewel' and third, an exquisite bloom of 'Dona Herzilia de Freitas Magalhaes', with a pronounced blue tinge. Fourth was Josephine Newman with 'Brushfield's Yellow'.

Class 18. This class for rose-formed or formal double cultivars attracted eight entries. First was Edmund de Rothschild with 'Laurel Leaf', 'William Bartlett' and a very lovely bloom of 'Pope John', a really beautiful full formal double in glistening white. Second came Josephine Newman with 'Cardinal Variegated', 'Commander Mulroy' and 'C. M. Hovey'. Third was Edmund de Rothschild with 'Mathotiana Alba', 'Joseph Pfingstl', and fourth, David Davis with 'Commander Mulroy', 'Matterhorn' and 'Diana's Charm', while A W Simons was highly commended for his entry of 'Wilamina', 'Nuccio's Cameo' and 'Commander Mulroy'.

Class 19. This class called for only one rose-formed or formal double cultivar and obtained 16 entries. First was Edmund de Rothschild, who showed 'Contessa Lavinia Maggi', second, Ann Hooton showing 'Berenice Perfection' and third, David Davis with 'Nuccio's Gem'. He also came fourth with 'William Bartlett'.

Class 20 is for any three cultivars other than those of *Camellia japonica*. The first entry by Ann Hooton was most outstanding, showing three superb blooms: 'Miss Tulare', 'Royalty' and 'Dr Clifford Parks'. Second came Mr A W Simons with 'Black Lace', 'Anticipation' and 'Otto Hopfer'. Third was Ann Hooton with 'Lasca Beauty', 'Francie L' and 'Leonard Messel' and fourth, Edmund de Rothschild with 'Anticipation', 'Elsie Jury' and 'Debbie'.

Class 21. This class for any *C. reticulata* species or hybrid produces some of the loveliest blooms, and there were nine entries. First was Ann Hooton with 'Dr Clifford Parks'. Second D R Strauss with 'Miles Rowell' and joint third, Ann Hooton with 'Royalty' and Edmund de Rothschild with 'Inspiration'.

Class 22 for any three *C. × williamsii*, one bloom of each, attracted 5 entries. First, Ann Hooton showing 'Anticipation', 'Bridal Gown' and 'Mona Jury'. Second, D R Strauss showing 'Mary Jobson', 'Jury's Yellow' and 'Debbie'. Third, Mr A W Simons showing 'Debbie', 'Elsie Jury' and 'Anticipation'.

Class 23 was for any single-flowered *C. × williamsii* cultivar. Again, five entries, one bloom. First, D R Strauss with 'Mary Jobson' and third, D R Strauss with 'Francis Hanger'.

Class 24. This class for one bloom of any semi-double *C. × williamsii* cultivar attracted seven entries. First came Mrs B Waterlow with 'Tip Toe', and second, D R Strauss with 'Charlean'.

Class 25 was more popular. It was for any anemone-formed or peony-formed *C. × williamsii* cultivar, one bloom, There were 11 entries. First was David Davis with 'Senorita', second, Ann Hooton with 'Elegant Beauty', third, Ann Hooton with 'Mona Jury' and fourth, D R Strauss with 'Debbie'.

Class 26. This class was for any rose-formed or formal double *C. × williamsii* cultivar. It attracted six entries. First was Ann Hooton with 'Julia Hamiter' (see Fig. 29), second, Edmund de Rothschild with 'E. G. Waterhouse' and third, Josephine Newman with 'Water Lily'.

Class 27 was for any species or hybrid not previously specified and of the six entrants two were successful. A W Simons was first with 'Scented Sun' and third with 'Spring Mist'. D R Strauss came second with *C. saluenensis*.

Finally, class 28, a most imaginative class requiring an arrangement of camellias shown for effect; one vase, space restricted to 75x75cm ((2 1/2 × 2 1/2ft), no other plant material to be used. A difficult assignment with camellias as the subject. There was one entry only from Ann Hooton, using 'Forest Green' and 'Emperor of Russia'. It was a most beautiful arrangement which well deserved a first but was assigned a second place; not a result to encourage what could be a most rewarding class when exhibitors become accustomed to realising it is included, as it is to be hoped it will, since it provides an entirely new dimension to the show.

Our sincere thanks to all the exhibitors. Without them there is no show and no competition. An especial thanks to Ann Hooton, Edmund de Rothschild, D R Strauss, David Davis, A W Simons and Josephine Newman for their continued support and to all the others who will have a chance next time.

Cicely Perring

AWARDS

Award of Merit

Rhododendron **'Caroline de Rothschild'** (['Repose' × 'Elizabeth de Rothschild'] × 'Stanway') AM 18 May 1998, as a hardy flowering plant for exhibition.
Loose truss of *c*.11 flowers, 180mm across. Flowers fragrant. Corolla funnel-campanulate 60 × 80mm, 7-lobed, dusky pink (47A) in bud, opening to creamy-white (4D) but slightly darker (to 6D) in throat, base of 3 dorsal lobes with greenish-yellow (151B) spotting and streaking extending out for ~20mm. Stamens 14, held within; filaments yellow-white; anthers brown. Style pale green, glandular throughout; stigma green; ovary green and glandular. Calyx same colour as corolla, petaloid and irregularly lobed, to 20mm. Pedicel glabrous, flushed red on upper surface. Leaves oblong, to 170 × 70mm, glabrous, matt green above, paler beneath; petiole to 25mm. Raised by Mr E de Rothschild. Exhibited by Mr E de Rothschild, Exbury Gardens, Exbury, Hampshire SO45 1AZ.

Rhododendron **'Milk Shake'** (['Repose' × 'Elizabeth de Rothschild'] × 'Stanway') AM 18 May 1998, as a hardy flowering plant for exhibition. Loose truss of *c*. 11 flowers, 200mm across. Flowers fragrant. Corolla funnel-campanulate, 70 × 110mm, 7-lobed, dusky pink (181C) in bud, opening to creamy-white (4D) deepening (to 5A) in throat with faint greenish spotting at base of dorsal lobes. Stamens 15, held within; filaments yellow-white; anthers brown. Style pale green, glandular throughout; stigma

green; ovary green and glandular. Calyx insignificant, to ~3mm. Pedicel slightly glandular, flushed red on upper surface. Leaves oblong, to 180 × 65mm, glabrous, matt green above, paler beneath; petiole to 25mm. Raised by Mr E de Rothschild. Exhibited by Mr E de Rothschild, Exbury Gardens, Exbury, Hampshire SO45 1AZ.

Rhododendron **'Pure Cream'** (*R. hyperythrum* × 'Crest'). AM 18 May 1998, as a hardy flowering plant for exhibition. Loose truss of *c*. 13 flowers, 160mm across. Corolla funnel-campanulate, 45 × 70mm, 6–7 rounded lobes, pale lemon-yellow (1D) with two faint green lines on dorsal surface inside. Stamens 12, held within; filaments yellow-white, hairy at base, anthers brown. Style pale green, few hairs at base; ovary green and glandular. Calyx green and very irregular, to 5mm. Pedicel glandular, green. Leaves elliptic, to 100 × 40mm, glabrous, mid-green above, yellowish green below; petiole to 20mm. Raised by Mr E de Rothschild. Exhibited by Mr E de Rothschild, Exbury Gardens, Exbury, Hampshire SO45 1AZ.

Rhododendron **'Mrs Marks'** ('Mrs G.W. Leak' × 'Stanway') AM 28 April 1998, as a hardy flowering plant for exhibition.
Loose, well-formed truss of *c*. 12 flowers, 180mm across. Corolla funnel-campanulate, 60 × 90mm, 5–6 lobed; lobes widely flaring and somewhat frilly, shorter than tube; bud reddish pink (53D), opening to pink (55A-B), upper corolla lobe with prominent flare of dark red (59A) markings extending from

base to within 20mm of lobe apex. Stamens *c.* 13, held free within; filaments white; anthers brown. Style exceeding stamens, yellowish-white, glandular at base; stigma red; ovary with glandular white hairs. Calyx rudimentary, 1–2mm. Pedicel with short glandular hairs, green with slight red flushing. Leaves elliptic, to 170 × 75mm, glabrous; petiole to 30mm. Raised by Mr E de Rothschild. Exhibited by Mr E de Rothschild, Exbury Gardens, Exbury, Hampshire SO45 1AZ.

***Rhododendron* 'Rajpur'** ('Jalisco' × 'Trianon') AM 28 April 1998, as a hardy flowering plant for exhibition.
Dome-shaped truss of *c.* 11 flowers, 130mm across. Flowers fragrant. Corolla funnel-campanulate 40 × 70mm, 7-lobed; lobes widely flaring and somewhat frilly, shorter than tube; bud pink (48B-C), opening to pale pink (38B-C) fading to greenish-yellow internally with a few faint green spots at base. Stamens 15; filaments greenish-white, hairy at base; anthers pale brown. Style exceeding stamens, yellowish white, glandular hairs throughout length; stigma olive green; ovary with glandular white hairs. Calyx irregular to 5mm. Pedicel green with sparse glandular hairs. Leaves oblong-elliptic to 140 × 60mm, somewhat glaucous beneath, glabrous; petiole to 30mm. Raised by Mr E de Rothschild. Exhibited by Mr E de Rothschild, Exbury Gardens, Exbury, Hampshire SO45 1AZ.

***Rhododendron* 'Solway'** ([*R. viscosum* × 'Sylphides'] × 'Sugared Almond') AM 24 May 1999, as a hardy flowering plant for exhibition.
A deciduous azalea (Ness Holt hybrid). Truss 8-flowered. Bud yellowish-pink (43C). Corolla 35 × 70mm, funnel-shaped with 5 broad, very spreading, slightly frilly lobes;

tube 20 × 6–7mm overlaid with pink (48B) and scattered bristly, non-glandular, 1–2mm hairs; lobes 35 × 30mm, light purplish-pink (62B) on front and back with diffuse white central band *c.* 5mm wide on inner surface, upper lobe with small 15 × 5mm 1 or 2 rayed orange (26B) flare. Stamens 5, *c.* 65mm, exserted, pink at base fading to white at apex, pubescent in lower half; anthers beige. Style slightly exceeding anthers and darker pink (47C); stigma capitate, dark green; ovary densely long-haired. Calyx lobes 1–2mm, green with slight red flush and scattered 1–2mm bristly hairs. Leaves not present at anthesis. Raised by E G Millais. Exhibited by Millais Nurseries, Crosswater Farm, Churt, Farnham, Surrey GU10 2JN.

***Rhododendron* 'White Perfume'** (Parentage unrecorded) AM 23 June 1998, as a hardy flowering plant for exhibition.
A deciduous azalea (Ness Holt hybrid). Truss of *c.* 13 flowers, 100mm across. Highly fragrant. Corolla 35 × 25mm, 5 lobed, funnel-shaped with long narrow tube, predominantly white with yellow and pink flush in bud; tube 25mm long, 4–5mm wide, retaining some pink at base externally; lobes 20 × 12mm, upper lobe with dull yellow (11A) flash; covered externally in long, white, red-tipped, glandular hairs. Stamens 5, protruding; filaments white, pubescent at base; anthers pale brown. Style protruding, white flushed pink, pubescent at base; stigma greenish-brown; ovary densely covered with glandular hairs. Calyx with 5 oblong, glandular, green lobes to 8mm. Pedicel strongly red-flushed, to 20mm, glandular hairy. Leaves (at anthesis) elliptic to obovate, to 45 × 15mm, glabrous above, margin and midrib below ciliate, apex acute, base cuneate; petiole very short. Raised by Denny Pratt. Exhibited by G Reuthe Ltd, Crown Point

Nursery, Sevenoaks Road, Ightham, Sevenoaks, Kent TN15 0HB.

***Rhododendron veitchianum* Cubittii Group 'Penelope Jack'** AM 16 February 1999, as a hardy flowering plant for exhibition.
Truss of 3 or 4 flowers. Fragrant. Corolla 80 × 100mm, 5 lobed, essentially white but with slight pink (48C) flushing on outer surface of tube; lobes 40 × 40mm, edges crisped; tube 40mm long, 10mm wide at base, 30mm wide at apex, pubescent at base on outside; inside of tube with a blotch 50–60 × 20mm of dense yellow-orange (16A) speckling. Calyx insignificant, 1–2mm, with scattered cilia to 5mm long. Stamens 10, 60–70mm long; filaments white, pubescent at base; anthers pale beige. Style 70mm, apex white, base green and scaly; stigma pale green and knobbly; ovary green, densely scaly. Pedicel 20mm, pale green with scattered green scales. Leaves elliptic, to 80 × 30mm, dark green above with scattered brown scales, pale green (almost glaucous) below with scattered brown scales. Margin of younger leaves retain 2mm ciliate bristles; petiole 5–10mm. Originator unknown. Exhibited by Dr R H L Jack, Edgemoor, Loch Road, Lanark, ML11 9BG.

***Rhododendron* seedling 210/3, provisional name 'Golden Comet'** AM, 28 April 1999, as a hardy flowering plant for exhibition.
Rounded truss of *c.* 12 flowers. Scented. Bud greyish-red (182B). Corolla widely funnel-shaped 40 × 70mm, 7-lobed, greenish-yellow (4A-B) inside and out with no internal or external markings. Stamens 14; filaments pale yellow; anthers pale brown. Style pale yellowish-green, glandular at base; ovary green, glandular. Calyx rudimentary with irregular lobes to 2mm. Pedicel 2 cm, slight-

ly glandular. Leaves hairless, oblong with rounded apex and rounded to cordate base, 110 × 55mm, matt mid-green above, slightly glaucous beneath; petiole *c.* 2.5cm, heavily flushed maroon. Raised by A F George. Exhibited by Hydon Nurseries, Clock Barn Lane, Hydon Heath, Godalming, Surrey GU8 4AZ.

First Class Certificate
***Rhododendroni* 'Tower Daring'** (*R. atlanticum* × unknown) FCC 24 May 1999, as a hardy flowering plant for exhibition.
A deciduous azalea (Cote hybrid). Dense trusses of up to 30 flowers. Bud deep pink (51B). Corolla funnel-shaped, 40 × 35mm, with 5 narrow lobes, strong pink (62A-B) with darker pink (54A) midribs and veining; tube 20mm long, 5mm wide at narrowest point, overlaid with pink (51B), shortly pubescent with scattered, longer hairs externally; lateral and lower lobes 30–35 × 12mm, upper lobe 20–25 × 15–20mm, with yellowish-orange (23B) flare 20 × 10mm. Stamens 5, *c.* 45mm, exserted, pink at base fading to white at apex, pubescent in lower half; anthers mid-brown. Style slightly exceeding anthers; ovary densely hairy. Calyx with irregular 1–2mm lobes, green, long white hairs. Pedicel 20mm with dark pink flush and scattered 1–2mm bristly hairs. Leaves (at anthesis) c. 60 × 25mm, obovate, margin and midrib on lower surface ciliate. Raised by J B Stevenson. Exhibited by Hydon Nurseries, Clock Barn Lane, Hydon Heath, Godalming, Surrey GU8 4AZ.

***Rhododendron* 'Stopham Lad'** FCC 22 June 1999, as a hardy flowering plant for exhibition.
A deciduous azalea. Tight, dome-shaped truss of *c.* 30 flowers. Fragrant. Bud creamy-white with corolla lobe midveins and tube

flushed reddish-pink (51B). Corolla funnel-shaped, 40 × 30mm, with 5 spreading lobes and covered externally with glandular hairs; tube 15 × 4mm, flushed reddish-pink (51A); lower 4 lobes 30 × 15mm, white but faintly flushed pink on inner surface and midvein reddish-pink (51B) on outer surface. Upper lobe 25 × 20mm with yellow (17B) blotch covering most of inner surface. Stamens 5, 45mm, exserted, pink at base fading to white at apex, pubescent in lower half; anthers mid-brown. Style 55mm, pinkish-red throughout; stigma capitate, lime green; ovary glandular pubescent. Calyx lobes 3–4mm, green with glandular pubescence. Pedicel 15mm, glandular-pubescent. Leaves elliptic to obovate, to 70 × 20mm at anthesis. Raised by M C Pratt. Exhibited by Mr J Harrington, The Upper Lodge, Stopham, Pulborough, West Sussex RH20 1EB.

BOOK REVIEW

Magnolia by Graham Rankin, 1999, Hamlyn, £14.99 (128pp)

Graham Rankin will be no stranger to members of the Group in the South East having been himself a Branch member. He has worked with two very fine collections of magnolias at Windsor and at Tilgates both of which the Group has visited. Thus his qualification to write this book is of the highest order as the result shows.

The Introduction is followed by History and Nomenclature, Plant Hunters, (mainly devoted to, and quoting extensively from, George Forrest) then Propagation containing sound advice on techniques for raising plants from seed, cuttings, grafting in its various forms, layering and micropropagation, which last is probably best left to the experts. There follows a particularly useful chapter on buying magnolias which sets out the various snags likely to be met and gives good down-to-earth advice on avoiding these. Planting and pruning are both covered in depth, the former including growing under glass. In the chapter dealing with pests and diseases it is interesting to note that the author has had success against honey fungus (*Armillaria*) even at an advanced state of infection – many gardeners will welcome his recipe for cure if not for the resultant smell in the garden.

The personal evaluation of not only the older species and cultivars but also the newer ones forms useful guidelines for the prospective purchaser. For those interested in associated plants the genera *Liriodendron*, *Mangletia* and *Michelia* are given coverage. The colour photographs (some 140 in all) are of excellent quality and were used in aid of the text for such matters as propagation etc are well chosen and clear.

In all an excellent book for both beginner and the more advanced alike written in plain terms by a hands-on gardener who knows what he is talking about. A good buy.

Bruce Archibold

RHS Rhododendron and Camellia Committee

Chairman
J D Bond, LVO, VMH, Georgia Lodge, Buckhurst Road, Cheapside, Ascot, Berks SL5 7RP

Vice-Chairmen
J T Gallagher, 2 Station Road, Verwood, Dorset BH31 6PU
J G Hillier, c/o Hillier Nurseries, Ampfield House, Ampfield, Hants SO51 9PA

Members
Lady Aberconway, Bodnant, Tal-y-Cafn, Colwyn Bay, Clwyd LL28 5RE
Lord Aberconway, VMH, Bodnant, Tal-y-Cafn, Colwyn Bay, Clwyd LL28 5RE
B Archibold, Starveacre, Dalwood, Axminster, East Devon EX13 7HH
The Hon. Edward Boscawen, Garden House, High Beeches Lane, Handcross, Sussex
    RH17 6HQ
M Flanagan, Keeper of the Gardens, The Great Park, Windsor, Berkshire SL4 2HT
A F George, Hydon Nurseries, Hydon Heath, Godalming, Surrey GU9 4AZ
Dr R Jack, Edgemoor, Loch Road, Lanark ML11 9BG
D G Millais, Crosswater Farm, Churt, Farnham, Surrey GU10 2JN
M Pharaoh, Marwood Hill, Marwood, Barnstaple, Devon EX31 4EB
A V Skinner, MBE, 2 Frog Firle Cottage, Alfriston, nr Polegate, E Sussex BN26 5TT
M O Slocock, VMH, Knap Hill Nursery, Knaphill, Woking, Surrey GU21 2JW
Maj. T le M Spring-Smyth, 1 Elcombe's Close, Lyndhurst, Hants SO43 7DS
O R Staples, York Gate, Back Church Lane, Adel, Leeds, W Yorks LS16 8DW
C Tomlin, Starborough Nursery, Starborough Road, Marsh Green, Edenbridge, Kent
    TN8 5RB
Miss J Trehane, Church Cottage, Hampreston, Wimborne, Dorset BH21 7LX
F J Williams, Caerhays Castle, Gorran, St Austell, Cornwall PL26 6LY
M Grant, RHS Garden Wisley (Secretary)

RHS Rhododendron, Camellia and Magnolia Group

Officers

Chairman Mr John BOND, LVO, VMH, Georgia Lodge, Buckhurst Road, Cheapside, Ascot, Berkshire SL5 7RP (Tel: 01344 625084)

Hon. Treasurer Mr Chris WALKER, 81 Station Road, Shepley, Huddersfield, W Yorks HD8 8DS (Tel: 01484 604922, Fax: 01484 602973)

Hon. Secretary Mrs Josephine M WARREN, Netherton, Buckland Monachorum, Yelverton, Devon PL20 7NL (Tel/fax: 01822 854022)

Hon. Membership Secretary Mr Tony WESTON, Whitehills, Newton Stewart, Scotland DG8 6SL (Tel: 01671 402049, Fax: 01671 403106, email: tony@rhodo.demon.co.uk)

Hon. Tours Organizer Vacant

Hon. Year Book Editor Mr Philip D EVANS, Painswold, Broad Street, Cuckfield, W Sussex RH17 5LL (Tel/fax: 01444 450788, email: evans@painswold.freeserve.co.uk)

Hon. Bulletin Editor Mrs Eileen WHEELER, Llwyngoras, Velindre, Crymych, Dyfed SA41 3XW (Tel: 01239 820464, email: e.wheeler@btinternet.com)

Committee Members

Mr David N FARNES, 5 Pine View (off Deerlands Road), Ashgate, Chesterfield, Derbyshire S40 4DN (Tel: 01246 272105)

Mr Martin D C GATES, 12 Marlborough Road, Chandlers Ford, Eastleigh, Hants SO53 5DH (Tel: 01703 252843)

Mr John D HARSANT, Newton House, Wall Lane, Heswell, Wirral, Merseyside L60 8NF (Tel: 0151 342 3664)

Dr R H L JACK, Edgemoor, Loch Road, Lanark ML11 9BG (Tel: 01555 663021)

Miss Cicely E PERRING, Watermill House, Watermill Lane, Pett, E Sussex TN35 4HY (Tel: 01424 812103)

Mr Alastair STEVENSON, 24 Bolton Road, Grove Park, London W4 3TB (Tel: 0181 742 7571, Fax: 0181 987 8728, email: stevensonmpa@compuserve.com)

Mr Ivor T STOKES, Pantcoch, Carmel, Llanelli, Dyfed SA14 7SG (Tel: 01269 844048)

Branch Chairmen

International Mr Michael JURGENS, The Old House, Silchester, Reading, Berkshire RG7 2LU (Tel: 01189 700240, Fax: 01189 701682)

N Ireland Mr Patrick FORDE, Seaforde, Downpatrick, Co Down BT30 8PG
   (Tel: 01396 811225, Fax: 01396 811370)
New Forest Mr Christopher FAIRWEATHER, The Garden Centre, High Street, Beaulieu,
   Hants SO42 7YR (Tel: 01590 612307, Fax: 01590 612519)
Norfolk Mrs J M IDIENS, Beaconswood, Roman Camp, Sandy Lane, West Runton,
   Cromer, Norfolk NR27 9ND (Tel: 01263 837779)
North Wales and Northwest Mr J Ken HULME, Treshnish, 72 Parkgate Road, Neston,
   S Wirral L64 6QQ (Tel: 0151 336 8852)
Peak District Mr David N FARNES, 5 Pine View (off Deerlands Road), Ashgate,
   Chesterfield, Derbyshire, S40 4DN (Tel: 01246 272105)
Southeast Mr John E HILLIARD, 99 Gales Drive, Three Bridges, Crawley, Sussex
   RH10 1QD (Tel: 01293 522859)
Southwest Dr Alun J B EDWARDS, 12 Ellerslie Road, Barnstaple, Devon, EX31 2HT
   (Tel: 01271 343324)
Wessex Mrs Miranda GUNN, Ramster, Petworth Road, Chiddingfold, Surrey GU8 4SN
   (Tel: 01428 644422)

Website address
http://www.rhs.org.uk/rhsgroups/memb.asp

WINDSOR GREAT PARK

SAVILL GARDEN

in Windsor Great Park
Situated in Wick Lane, Englefield Green, Surrey (off A30)
Signposted from Ascot, Egham (M25) & Windsor (M4)

Created within Windsor Great Park by Sir Eric Savill this beautiful garden is an oasis of tranquility. Come and discover its secrets and surprises - relax in our spacious restaurant and enjoy a peaceful browse in our gift/plant shop.

Open daily 10-6pm. For further information please call the Crown Estate Office 01753 847518

INDEX

Abies fargesii 35
Abies koreana 65
Acer campbellii 28
Acer pseudoplatanus
  'Simon-Louis Frères' 64
Acer sikkimense 35
Acer wardii 35
Aesculus assamica 28
Aesculus × mutabilis
  'Induta' 64
Aesculus pavia
  'Atrosanguinea' 64
Alnus glutinosa
  'Imperialis' 66
Alnus nepalensis 33
Altingia excelsa 33
Arbutus unedo 66
Azalea rustica plena 62
Bucklandia populnea
  28,33,34
Camellia
  Adelina Patti 76
  Adolphe Audusson
    47,74,76
  Alba Simplex 76
  Annabel Lansdell 75
  Annie Wylam 75,76
  Anticipation 47,75,77
  Augusto L'Gouveia
    Pinto 74
  Augusto Pinto 12,75
  Barbara Mary 76
  Berenice Perfection
    75,77
  Black Lace 77
  Blaze of Glory 47
  Bob Hope 76
  Bowbells 47
  Bridal Gown 47,77
  Brigadoon 47
  Brushfield's Yellow
    47,75,76
  Buddha 11
  Burgundy Gem 76
  C M Wilson 74
  C. M. Hovey 76
  Cameo 74
  Cardinal Variegated
    75,76
  Carolyn Snowdon 11
  Carter's Sunburst 74
  Charlean 76,77
  Cheryl Lynn 74
  chrysantha 75
  Clarissa 74,76
  Commander Mulroy 76

Camellia (cont.)
  Contessa Lavinia Maggi
    47,77
  controversa 64
  cuspidata 47
  Debbie 9,11,47,75,77
  Desire 75
  Diana's Charm 75,76
  Diatorin 76
  Dixie Knight 74
  Dona Herzilia de Freitas
    Magalhaes 74,76
  Donation 9,10,47,66
  Dr Burnside Variegated
    76
  Dr Clifford Parks 75,77
  Dr Tinsley 74
  Drama Girl 10,74,75,76
  Dream Girl 47
  E. G. Waterhouse 11,77
  Elegans 47,76
  Elegans Champagne 76
  Elegans Splendor 76
  Elegant Beauty 77
  Elizabeth de Rothschild
    75
  Elizabeth Dowd 76
  Elsie Jury 11,47,75,77
  Emperor of Russia
    74,77
  Evelyn 76
  Extravaganza 76
  Faith 74,76
  Forest Green 77
  Francie L 9,75,77
  Francis Hanger 47,77
  Furo-An 74
  Grand Prix 75,76
  Grand Slam 12,74
  Haku Rakuten 74
  Hanatachi Bama 76
  Harold Paige 12
  Hatsu Sakura 76
  Hawaii 76
  Henry Turnbull 76
  Hilda Jamieson 75
  Hope 47
  Howard Asper 12
  Inspiration 12,47,75,77
  japonica 50,76
    'Betty Sheffield
      Supreme' 10
    'Cornish Snow' 47,66
    'Cornish Spring' 47
    'Donckelaari' 50
    'Guilio Nuccio' 11,76

Camellia japonica (cont.)
  'Masayoshi' 50
  'Mrs D.W. Davis' 12,
    47,76
  'Nuccio's Jewel'
    64,75,76
  'Scentsation' 11
  'Ville de Nantes' 11
  'White Nun' 9,12
  Japonica Bonetsu 76
  Jennifer Turnbull 76
  Jessica Kaby 74
  Joan Trehane 47
  Joseph Pfingstl 76
  Joshua Youtz 74
  Julia Drayton 74
  Julia Hamiter 75,77
  Juno 76
  Jupiter 76
  Jury's Yellow 47,75,77
  Kelvingtonia 76
  Kitty 12
  Kramer's Supreme
    74,75,76
  Lady Clare 47,76
  Lady Lock 74
  Lasca Beauty 77
  Laurel Leaf 76
  Lavinia 76
  Leonard Messel
    47,75,77
  Leonora Novick 74
  Lily Pons 75
  Little Bit 76
  lutchuensis 12
  Madge Miller 74
  Maggi 76
  Mandalay Queen 12,75
  Margaret Davis
    9,12,75,76
  Margaret Rose 74
  Mary Jobson 75,77
  Mary Larcom 75
  Mary Taylor 75
  Masayoshi 50
  Matador 9
  Mathotiana 12
  Mathotiana Alba 47,76
  Mathotiana Supreme 74
  Matterhorn 75,76
  Midnight 76
  Miles Rowell 77
  Miss Tulare 75,77
  Mona Jury 75,77
  Mouchang 9
  Muskoka 12

Camellia (cont.)
  My Darling 11
  Nicky Crisp 75
  Night Rider 76
  Nuccio's Cameo 76
  Nuccio's Gem 75,77
  Nuccio's Pearl 75,76
  Onetia Holland 76
  Otto Hopfer 75,77
  Owen Henry 76
  Pink Hellebore 11
  Pope John 75,76
  Powder Puff 74
  Premier 74
  Primavera 76
  Quintesscience 75
  R. L. Wheeler 75,76
  Red Cardinal 76
  reticulata 44,47,75,77
    'Buddha' 11
  Rosea 76
  Rosetsu 74
  Rosina Sobeck 11
  Royalty 75,77
  Rubescens 75
  Ruby Bells 75
  saluenensis 75,77
  San Dimas 12
  Satan's Robe 75
  Scented Sun 77
  Senorita 76,77
  Serenade 74
  sinensis 30,52
  Sir Victor Davis 76
  Souzas Pavlova 75
  Spring Festival 12
  Spring Mist 12,77
  St Ewe 47
  Strawberry Parfait 74
  Swan Lake 76
  Taro Kaya 75
  Tiffany 74,75
  Tip Toe 77
  Tom Thumb 76
  Tomorrow 75
  tsai 9
  Vallee Knudsen 9,75
  Water Lily 11,47,77
  Waterloo 76
  Wilamina 76
  Wilber Foss 75
  Wildfire 74,76
  Wildlife 74
  William Bartlett 76,77
  × *williamsii* 47,75,77
Clethra delavayi 35

Cornus
  alternifolia 64
  controversa 64
  florida 'Cherokee Chief'
    64
Crinodendron hookerianum
  64
Cryptomeria japonica 51
Davidia involucrata 64
Drimys winteri 65
Duabanga sonneratioides
  28,33
Erythrina indica 33
Eucalpytus nitens 65
Eucryphia 'Nymansay' 47
Ficus
  benjamina 28
  pyriformis 29
Gomer Waterer 42
Helicia excelsa 34
Homonoia riparia 29
Ilex
  latifolia 64
  nothofagifolia 35
  sikkimense 35
Keteleeria davidiana 64
Lilium Martagon 33
Gmelina arborea 33
Gordonia axillaris 34
Magnolia
  acuminata 20
  Alba Superba 46
  Alexandrina 46
  Ann Rosse 22
  Ann 46
  Arnold Dance 22
  Betty 46
  biondii 19
  Blood Moon 21
  brooklynensis
    'Woodsman' 46
  Brozzoni 46
  Burgundy 46
  Burncoose 20
  Buzzard 22
  Caerhays Belle 20
  campbellii 22,35,46,66
    var. *alba* 22
    subsp. *mollicomata* 22
      'Lanarth' 22
      'Werrinton' 52
  Chyverton 22
  Claret Cup 20
  Clarke 22
  Copeland Court 20
  Crimson Stipple 46
  cylindrica 19
  dawsoniana 22,46
  denudata 22
  denudata var. *elongata*
    20

Magnolia (cont.)
  Eric Savill 20
  Flamingo 20
  fraseri 66
  Galaxy 20
  globosa 23,46
    var. *sinensis* 23
  grandiflora 24
  Halesia carolina 46
  Hawk 22
  Heaven Scent 46
  hypoleuca 23,66
  Iolanthe 46
  Jane 46
  Joe McDaniel 46
  Judy 46
  kobus 21,46
  Lanhydrock 20
  Lennei 20,46
  liliflora 20
  liliiflora 'Nigra' 20, 46
  Manchu Fan 46
  Marj Gossler 22
  Mark Jury 22,46
  Marwood Spring 20
  Michael Rosse 22
  Mossman's Giant 22
  Multipetal 21
  nicholsoniana 22
  officinalis 24
    var. *biloba* 46
  Paul Cook 20
  Peachy 20
  Philip Tregunna 22
  Pinkie 20
  Princess Margaret 22
  Randy 46
  Raspberry Swirl 20
  Ricki 46
  Rosea 46
  rostrata 35
  Ruby Rose 22
  Rustica Rubra 46
  salicifolia 46
  San Jose 46
  sargentiana 21,22
    var. *robusta* 20,21,22,
      46,53,66
  sieboldii 23,46
    subsp. *sieboldii* 23
  sinensis 23,45,46
  Spectrum 20
  sprengeri 19
    'Diva' 19,20
    var. *diva* 46,66
    var. *elongata* 20
  × *soulangeana* 46
  Star Wars 46
  stellata 'Rosea' 46
  Susan 46
  Treve Holman 22

Magnolia (cont.)
  Ursula Grau 23
  Valley Splendour 22
  × *veitchii* 66
  wilsonii 22,23,46
  Yellow Bird 46
  Yellow Fever 46
Manglietia insignis 28,33
Meliosma myriantha 64
Mesua ferrea 33
Metasequoia glyptostroboides
  63,66
Michelia montana 28
Myrica nagei 28
Myrtus luma 65
Nothofagus antartica 66
Nothofagus fusca 64
Nyssa sylvatica 62
Olearia scilloniensis 65
Phoenix canariensis 51
Pinus montezumae
  62,64,65
Pinus patula 66
Primula petiolares 35
Prunus cerasoides 28
Prunus sargentii 54
Quercus myrsinifolia 63
Quercus oxyclodon 64
Rhabdia lycioides 29
Rhododendron
  aberconwayi 69
  adenogynum 68
  Amanda Sue 64
  amoenum 70
  Androcles 68
  Angelo 5,62
  anthosphaerum 68
  anweiense 69
  Apricot Fantasy 41
  arboreum 16,32,57,67
    var. *roseum* 67
  argipeplum 14,15,16
  argyrophyllum 'Chinese
    Silver' 69
  arizelum 35,42,69
  atlanticum 80
  augustinii 70
  auriculatum 45,73
  Bagshot Sands 45
  baileyi 70
  barbatum 14,15,16,45
  Beauty of Littleworth
    71
  Biskra 72
  Blewbury 72
  Blue Peter 62
  Bob's Choice 73
  Bow Bells 72
  bureavii 41,45
  burmanicum 44,70
  Calfort Bounty 71,72

Rhododendron (cont.)
  calophytum 3,64,67
  calostrotum 40
  caloxanthum 52
  Cameo Spico 68
  campanulatum 57,69,73
  campylocarpum 68
  campylocarpum ×
    'Idealist' 63
  campylogynum 'Bodnant
    Red' 45
  Carita Inchmery 72
  Caroline de Rothschild
    78
  catawbiense 57
  caucasicum 70
  cephalanthum 45
  christianae 68
  Chrysomanicum 68
  Churchill 70
  Cilpinense 68
  cinnabarinum 40,70
  Colonel Rogers 72
  coriaceum 69
  Cornish Cross 72
  Cornish Red 63
  Cornubia 68
  Countess of Athlone 71
  Crest 78
  cubittii 70
  Curlew 40
  dalhousiae 44
  David Rockefeller 72
  davidsonianum 69
  decorum 69
  dendricola 33
  denudatum 40
  diaprepes 53
  dichroanthum 41
    subsp. *scyphocalyx* 66
  Doncaster 71
  Dora Amateis 73
  Dr Albert Schweitzer 41
  Duchess of Kent 73
  eclecteum 35
  edgworthii 72
  Egret 71
  elegantulum 45
  Elizabeth de Rothschild
    78
  erosum 14,15,17
  exasperatum 14,17
  faberi 70
  Fairylight 41
  falconeri 46,70,73
    subsp. *eximium* 67
  fastigiatum 40
  Fastuosum Flore-Pleno
    71
  fictolacteum 66,69
  First Light 69

Rhododendron (cont.)
 flinckii 40
 Floradora 73
 Fortune 70,73,74
 fortunei 3,72
 Fragrantissimum 44,72
 fulgens 40
 fulvum 68,69
 Furnival's Daughter 73
 Gamechick 45
 genestierianum 34
 Ginny Gee 71
 Gipsy King 72
 Giraldii 68
 glaucophyllum 69,70
 glischrum subsp.
    glischroides 67
 Glory of Penjerrick 68
 Golden Comet 80
 grande 68
 griersonianum 72
 griffithianum 57,69
 haematodes 70,71
 Halfdan Lem 73
 Hawk Crest 63,71
 heliolepis 40
 Hermione Knight
    71,72
 himantodes 70
 Hinodegiri 73
 hippophaeoides 70
 hodgsonii 68
    'Poet's Lawn' 69
 horlickianum 44
 huianum 40
 hylaeum 68
 hyperythrum 78
 Iceberg 45
 Idealist 63,71
 imberbe 16
 insigne 42
 irroratum 63,68
 Ivery's Scarlet 68
 Jalisco 79
 Janet 68
 jasminiflorum 70
 javanicum 73
 Jessica de Rothschild 71
 johnstonianum 70
 Julie 45
 Just Peachy 68
 Karkov 72
 kesangiae 45
 Kilimanjaro 73
 King George 45

Rhododendron (cont.)
 kingianum 73
 kiusianum 50
 Koichiro Wada 45
 Lady Alice Fitzwilliam
    72
 laetum 73
 Lamellen 71,72
 lanigerum 67
 lindleyi 44
 Little Pinkie 69
 Loderi 63
 Loderi King George 71
 Loderi Sir Joseph
    Hooker 71
 Loderi Venus 71
 Loders White 71
 loranthiflorum 70
 ludlowii 45
 Luscombei 72
 lutescens 'Bagshot Sands'
    45
 luteum 64
 macabeanum
    45,46,64,67,68
 macrosmithii 14,15,16
 makinoi 42
 mallotum 45
 Mariloo 72
 Matador 72
 maximum 57
 May Day 72
 meddianum 67
 Merganiser 71
 metternichii 70
 Milk Shake 78
 Montreal 70
 moulmainense 34
 Mrs Furnival 71
 Mrs G.W. Leak 71,78
 Mrs Marks 78
 Naomi Nautilus 72
 neriiflorum 40
 nervulosum 70
 New Comet 52
 nishiokae 17
 niveum 68,69
    Crown Equerry 52
 Nobleanum Album 68
 Noyo Chief 73
 obtusum f. *amoenum*
    var. *coccineum* 64
 ochraceum 40
 Olga 41
 Orange Beauty 73

Rhododendron (cont.)
 orbiculare 69,71,72
 oreodoxa 45,67
    var. *fargesii* 67
    var. *oreodoxa* 67
 orthocladum 40
 Ottawa 70
 Our Kate 68
 pachysanthum 45
 Papaya Punch 41
 Penelope Jack 80
 Percy Wiseman 64
 piercei 68
 Pink Coral 63
 Pink Delight 68,73
 Pink Diamond 45
 Polar Bear 45
 polyandrum 35
 ponticum 44,57
    'Silver Edge' 41
 praestans 45
 praevernum 45
 primuliflorum 40
 principis 68
 pumilum 45
 Pure Cream 78
 Queen of Hearts 71,73
 racemosum 67,68
 Rajpur 79
 ramsdenianum 45
 Red Carpet 40
 Repose 78
 rhabdotum 44
 rhombicum 70
 Rosie Posie 69
 roxieanum 69,70,72
 Roza Stevenson 71,72
 Rubicon 73
 rubiginosum 70
 Ruby Hart 71
 sargentianum
    'Whitebait' 45
 Scarlet Wonder 40
 seinghkuense 69
 serpyllifolium 63
 Seven Stars 72
 Shantung Rose 73
 Shilsonii 68
 Shin-seikai 73
 sidereum 42
 siderophyllum 68
 simsii 27
 sinogrande 35,45,70,73
 Sir Edmund 63
 smirnowii 41,69

Rhododendron (cont.)
 smithii 14,15,16
 Solway 79
 Souvenire de Dr Endtz
    71
 sphaeroblastum 70
 spinuliferum 63,64
 St Tudy 72
 Stanley 70
 Stanway 78
 stenaulum 34
 Stopham Lad 80
 strigillosum 45,67
 succothii 14,16,17
 Sugared Almond 79
 Susan 71
 sutchuenense 45,68
 Sylphides 79
 taggianum 'Harry Tagg'
    52
 tanastylum 68
 telopeum 35
 tephropeplum 35
 Terracotta 41
 Tower Daring 80
 Trianon 79
 trichocladum 35,40
 Tropical Fanfare 73
 tyermannii 72,73
 uvarifolium 67,68
 Venus 45
 Vienna 71
 viscosum 79
 wasonii 68
 W.F.H. 71
 Wee Bee 40
 Werei 68
 White Glory 63
 White Perfume 79
 White Wings 71
 wightii 69
 williamsianum 72
 wiltonii 40
 yakushimanum
    3,6,41,45,50,64,72

Rhodoleia forrestii 34
Rosa bracteata 29
Salix tetrasperma 29
Terminalia myriocarpa
    28,33
Toddalia aculeata 33
Viburnum betulifolium 65
Viburnum macrocephalum
    65

It's Somewhere You've Dreamed Of

Come and discover Exbury Gardens, where natural beauty is found at every corner. The world famous displays of rhododendrons, azaleas and camellias form a riot of colour and many rare specimens can be found within the 200 acre grounds. With an excellent plant centre, gift shop and catering facilities to help you enjoy your visit, Exbury is truly a memorable day out!

Open daily 10am - 5.30pm (Spring, Summer & Autumn)
Near Beaulieu, 20 minutes from M27 Junction 2
Telephone enquiries: (023) 80891203/80899422
Website: http://www.exbury.co.uk

EXBURY
—GARDENS—

GLENDOICK GARDENS LTD
PERTH PH2 7NS

TEL. 01738 860205
FAX. 01738 860630

e mail sales@glendoick.com

70 PAGE CATALOGUE WITH FULL DESCRIPTIONS. Send £1.50 (or £1 in stamps).

We currently propagate around 1000 different rhododendron and azalea species and cultivars plus many other plants, including Primula and Meconopsis. Many plants are from wild seed and several are newly introduced. We export. Mail order October-April 1st only.

SPECIES

Recent expeditions to N.E. Yunnan and S.E. Sichuan have introduced new species offered for the first time. These include the magnificent *R. glanduliferum* with scented white flowers and brightest red new growth, *R. denudatum, R. huianum, R. asterochnoum,* and *R. longipes* are all tough species which should make fine garden plants. From S. Yunnan, we have *R sinofalconeri* which should have yellow flowers to rival those of *R. macabeanum*. We have good stocks of other recently introduced and rare species such as *R. dendrocharis-* a miniature version of *R. m upinense* with deep pink flowers and a neat habit- and *R. proteoides* the connoisseur's species with small leaves and a very compact habit. For the conservatory or the milder southern or western garden, we have many wonderful species and hybrids. The rare *R. liliiflorum* is useful for its late-flowering as well as its white scented flowers. We also have good stocks of *R. seinghkuense* which is a yellow-flowered epiphyte, closely related to *R. edgeworthii.*

NEW HYBRIDS

The latest in the 'birds' series of dwarf hybrids are the bright-pink flowered 'Pintail' which is easy and vigorous and 'Crane' which is a creamy-white version of the popular 'Ginny Gee' We have just introduced the very fine, compact and hardy 'Frost Hexe' w ich is a purple daphne-flowered hybrid of *R. anthopogon x R. lapponicum.* Some of the best new larger hybrid introductions include our low yellows 'Loch Rannoch' and 'Loch of the Lowes' and the American and Canadian introductions: 'Elsie Watson', 'Ring of Fire', 'Midnight Mystique', 'Vineland Fragrance'

DECIDUOUS AZALEA SPECIES

More and more popular every year, these are grown for their scent and or relatively late flowering. For scent, try *R. atlanticum, R. arborescens,* and for scent and later flowering, try *R. occidentale* and *R. viscosum.*

INDOOR RHODODENDRONS

We have a huge range of Maddenia species and hybrids for mild gardens and conservatories. We also stock a good range of Vireya species and hybrids.

OTHER PLANTS

We stock a good range of asiatic primulas and meconopsis, many of which are grown from our own wild collections. We have a fine selection of *Kalmia latifolia* cultivars. Why not start a collection of *Sorbus* species to brighten up late summer and autumn. We have many rare and newly introduced species.

GLENDOICK GARDEN CENTRE

Perth-Dundee rd. Open 7 days a week.

tel 01738 860 260

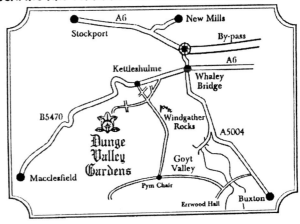

Rhododendrons & Azaleas

FOR THE CONNOISSEUR FROM **LODER PLANTS**

MAIL ORDER, PLANT CENTRE & EXPORT. TEL:**01403-891412** FAX **891336**.
SEND 2 x1ST STAMPS FOR AVAILABILITY LIST OR VIST OUR WEBSITE AT **www.rhododendrons.com**
OPEN BY APPOINTMENT ONLY. THIS IS SO WE CAN GIVE YOU OUR UNDIVIDED ATTENTION & ADVICE
**(OVER 1000 HYBRIDS, SPECIES AND AZALEAS, EVERGREEN OR DECIDUOUS, EARLY OR LATE
FLOWERING, SCENTED) & ACERS, CAMELLIA'S, MAGNOLIAS AND MANY OTHER CHOICE PLANTS**

JUST SOUTH OF

We're sure you'll enjoy a day at Leonardslee so much you'll invest in a season ticket and return again and again! The many miles of walks provide never ending delights and a changing landscape throughout the seasons. There are plenty of quiet spots where you can sit and enjoy one of England's greenest and most pleasant landscapes. The walks extend round the peaceful lakes and waterfalls where wildlife thrives.

Escape from the busy world in Leonardslee's tranquil 240 acres and enjoying the high variety of natural habitats. Watch the large carp in the Waterfall lake and glimpse wallabies and deer in their idyllic setting. Don't miss the Alpine House and Bonsai Exhibition, with lunch or tea in the Clock Tower Restaurant, and before you leave, browse around the good selection of plants for sale at the nursery.

Enjoy the Autumnal glory of Leonardslee where Maples and deciduous Azaleas take on their dramatic shades against the golds and russets of fine woodland trees. Liquidambars, Hickories and Tupelos provide shades of copper and gold. From mid-September until late October the colours change every week. The end of the season can be as dramatic as the beginning

LOWER BEEDING, HORSHAM, W.SUSSEX RH13 6PP. TEL: 01403 891212 FAX: 891305

SLOCOCK & KNAP HILL NURSERIES

Winner of the Rothschild Challenge Cup in 1997

RHODODENDRONS & AZALEAS

GROWERS FOR GENERATIONS

28 GOLD MEDALS AT THE CHELSEA FLOWER SHOW AND A GOLD MEDAL AT THE 1997 RHODODENDRON SHOW

Our catalogue/price list
is available by post from
Dept L, KNAP HILL NURSERY LTD.

Send 3 x 1st class stamps

Personal callers welcome by appointment.

SLOCOCK & KNAP HILL NURSERIES
Barrs Lane, Knaphill, Woking, Surrey GU21 2JW
Tel. 01483 481214 FAX 01483 797261
NURSERY OPEN 9am – 5pm MONDAY/FRIDAY
But CLOSED at weekends and Bank Holidays

Hydon Nurseries

Specialist growers of Rhododendrons, Azaleas, Camellias & Magnolias.

New Rhododendron catalogue now available -
price £1.50 (inc. postage) U.S.A. $5.00 (inc. air post)
We have an excellent selection of dwarf-growing varieties
and many species grown under Collectors' numbers.

We are pleased to undertake the export of plants and scions.
Rare plants propagated to order.
Visit our Rhododendron woodland and show garden.
Our Nursery is open from Monday to Saturday from 8am to 5pm
(Closed Saturday afternoons in June, July, Aug., Sept., Dec., Jan., & Feb.)

Clock Barn Lane, Hydon Heath, Godalming, Surrey, GU8 4AZ
Telephone: (01483) 860252
Fax: (01483) 419937